IN THIS remarkable book, Rudolf Schwarz, master builder of churches, discusses the questions facing those who seek to build true churches in our own time. He is a man entitled to speak with authority. Over sixty churches in Germany are living witnesses to the power of his conception and the brilliance of his execution. The best known of these, St. Elizabeth's at Mülheim, has been widely praised as the most successful architectural realization of the Christian spirit in modern times.

Schwarz speaks to the architect or congregation who see in the living entity of the church their architectural task. He addresses those who hope that their churches may be fit "bodies" for the "soul" of their congregations, for those who hope that their new churches may stand in the oldest as well as the newest traditions of religious building.

The early Christian and medieval churches truly expressed the spirit of their times; but since they represent a way of life that no longer exists, the old materials and designs are obsolete. Yet, whatever the era, the basic model for church building is the form of the human body: its form in space, which we all share, which Christ assumed and in which he suffered; and its form in time which led him, as it leads each Christian, from cradle to cross. Schwarz

RUDOLF SCHWARZ

helps us to realize the full consequences of the fact that the classical patterns are not frozen in the past, but fluid today, and hence he encourages us to unlock their wealth in answer to the challenge given us by our own time.

Accompanying the text with a series of drawings which illustrate the architectural possibilities inherent in natural and classical forms, Schwarz discusses the seven possible plans for the church building.

Schwarz' success with ecclesiastical architecture arises in part from his understanding of the church in its relation to the entire Christian community. Until 1951 he was director in charge of planning the reconstruction of war-devastated Cologne. One of his outstanding achievements was the rebuilding of the Gürzenich hall, around which the secular activities of the city have been centered since medieval times.

THE CHURCH INCARNATE

The Church Incarnate

The Sacred Function of Christian Architecture

RUDOLF SCHWARZ

TRANSLATED BY CYNTHIA HARRIS

HENRY REGNERY COMPANY · CHICAGO

Published as Vom Bau Der Kirche:
Verlag Lambert Schneider, Heidelberg, 1938

Contents

Foreword

THIS BOOK was written in Germany's darkest hour, but it throws light for the first time on the question of church building, and illuminates the whole problem of architecture itself.

Rudolf Schwarz, the great German church builder, is one of the most profound thinkers of our time. His book, in spite of its clarity, is not easy reading—but he who will take the trouble to study it carefully will gain real insight into the problems discussed. I have read it over and over again, and I know its power of clarification. I believe it should be read not only by those concerned with church building but by anyone sincerely interested in architecture. Yet it is not only a great book on architecture, indeed, it is one of the truly great books—one of those which have the power to transform our thinking.

I have always felt it should be translated into English. Now, thanks to Cynthia Harris, it can be studied by anyone in the English speaking world.

MIES VAN DER ROHE

Translator's Invitation

INTRODUCTIONS *are frequently useless—one misses nothing if one leaves them unread. But this book is of a particular, even of a difficult kind. It is itself an introduction, or more accurately an invitation. And so it will perhaps be helpful to provide it, as it were, with an invitation to its invitation.*

Mr. Schwarz' book makes one demand on its readers: it asks to be read with child-like innocence. Today it is difficult for us to approach any book with a calm mind and an open heart. As you read this page you have all the raw materials at hand which you will need for understanding this work. You are probably sitting in a chair—with the sun streaming over your shoulder, let us hope, or at least with a lamp at your side. With your hand you hold this book and your eye is running over the page. If you stop to think of it you have a spine which allows you to sit erect and ribs which allow you to breathe, giving you time for the reading. You will find yourself examining your body, feeling its powers and strengths, its weaknesses and limitations. And you will find yourself discovering new connections and relationships between your own body and those of other people. Therefore it would probably be best if you were to read this book aloud, since it is not only about your own body but also about that world in which we live where no body is alone, where no hand is meant to be left unclasped, no eye meant to miss that glimpse of the soul in the depths of another—about this world in which we ourselves can find our true life only as parts of the greater Body whose limbs we are, in time and in space.

CYNTHIA HARRIS

Spring, 1958
Munich, Germany

PART I
The Foundation

The Foundation

THE ALTAR was called "Christ" in former times, just as many other things were called "Christ" or "the body of Christ": the congregation or the house in which it gathered or, very generally, the earth. This was meant so literally that the individual parts of the house were compared to the individual limbs of his body, the nave with the trunk, the transept with the outspread arms and the choir with the head. Thus Christ hung perpetually on the cross, and because he bowed his head in death, as the Gospel relates, the choir was sometimes built at an angle to the nave. And so within this image—which was far more than a comparison—it would be fitting to call the altar the head or the heart of the Lord. And this was surely the intention.

It is hard for modern men to take such ideas seriously. Usually it is objected that they were based on false concepts of life, that the levels were confused, that reality and image were not kept distinct. There may be some truth in this. Still it must be retorted that the medieval concept of life was not a naive one and that, in the assertion that this or that "is" the body, the little word "is" remains completely open and is ready to exist at the most varied levels. The decisive reason for the modern objection cannot lie here.

Now it is certain that the Middle Ages knew how to build churches and that their churches were true churches. In this respect we have not surpassed them in the least. And so it is well to assume that their theoretical concepts cannot have been entirely false either.

Actually what separates us from these early teachings is not so much their content as the difference of language. Today we no longer connect the same images with the words and we put a new meaning into the old terms. When men spoke of the "body" or of the "body of Christ" in earlier times, they probably meant something quite different from what we mean when we speak about our body. And so to begin with we must try to make clear to ourselves what medieval men saw as "body."

This can be quite readily recognized in the early pictures which show the body in its holiness. The bodies are shown as something radiant and all the most brilliant colors are used for them, all the colors of glowing, burning things. And the head is enveloped in the "halo" as if in a radiant sun.

There is a hierarchy of colors in these pictures, culminating in the brightest white, and the gold is then the eternal light in which the saints are bathed.

The pictures also show the body condemned and rejected, usually in the form of an animal: it has taken on claws and beaks and the like or has been completely transformed into a monster. There is an order of the condemned colors, too, ending in a flame, the flame of an evil, inwardly-burning fire. And the abysmal darkness into which all this is sunk is the darkness of damnation, not the blackness of the sheltering night about the babe in the manger.

These pictures clearly showed that the holy body is something luminous, something star-like, and it is obvious that an eternal meaning was ascribed to the colors—in the mandorla of color the true essence found expression. And people believed that the luminous power of the body could be perverted and turned into its evil opposite. Here we are reminded that the Scripture tells of similar things, for instance when it relates that the Lord's face "shone" or Stephen's—in the latter's case it adds the explanation that he was looking up into the "wide open heaven."

In the Strasbourg tympanum, where the death of the Virgin is represented, the likeness of her dying body is escaping out of it and the Lord already holds this likeness in his hand. This is what is lasting: the body of the soul or the soul of the body. It is exactly like the corpse itself except that it is much smaller—but this does not mean that it is unimportant or only a left-over: it means that this is the intrinsic reality, the essence of body which, although it is not bound to any particular size, is indeed bound to the structural laws of bodily form and bodily growth.

The magnificent portal at Autun depicts the Last Judgment. The Lord is of mighty stature and is seated between heaven and earth to separate the living from the dead. Mary is also very large and the angels are only slightly smaller. These great angels are raising the people out of their graves, and the people are so small that it is hard to believe that all this is for them and their judgment. But the "souls" or the "spirits" are not depicted, for that would have been against the belief in the resurrection of the flesh. These are real men with real bodies who are climbing out of their graves, and this is the real Lord, the Lord whose incarnation in the flesh and in history the Christians have always taken so terribly literally. But if the Lord appears tremendous and mighty this can only mean that he has a mighty body and men a modest one.

There are many such representations of sacred history and they should be taken seriously. What they show is not meant as a landscape of the soul nor as an artistic interpretation—it is meant to be genuine history. Apparently in the course of this no one reflected on the fact that all the people should actually be shown with bodies of approximately the same size. The painters saw history from the center point of an absolute perspective, similar to the way in which God sees it, and within this perspective of very essence the differences in size arose by themselves. When, later on, the school of historical painting developed, the early art of painting history was lost. Painting continued to be done in perspective, but this new perspective was developed from a completely accidental standpoint and all the things were given in relation to it. The thing which happened to lie right next to this accidental point, were it only the tail-end of a horse, became immense. The school of historical painting moved the center of history out of God, but it did not transfer it to a great and important person, to a king, for instance, or to the leader in a battle—it simply moved it anywhere, into the arbitrary. Historical painting lost the center of history and then disintegrated into idle gossip. This is a comfortable art; or perhaps we should call it a highly difficult un-art, since it presupposes a singular and complex disturbance which no longer even sees what the pagan mythologies could see: that the great are great and the lesser small. (How splendidly the Edda builds a world for itself out of a few figures and their great works—a few men, a tree, a wolf, a snake, a bridge and the like. And is not a city such as Mycaenae similarly designed, with its few glorious elements, the grave, the gateway, the street, the hall?)

In earlier times men must have seen the community itself like this.

Troubetzkoy, who speaks so beautifully about the holy fire burning in the ancient icons, speaks, too, about the old Russian cities. The "onion dome" has nothing to do with either an onion or a dome. It is the flame, he says, and when one sees such an old city, lying with her many churches sunlit upon the open plain, the earth is afire. The city is a sea of flame.

The structure of our own cities in Europe was little different. The houses were small and were consumed in the flames of the great spires.

If we gather a large number of such things out of art, out of the lives of the saints and also out of the teachings—for instance the teaching about the transfigured body—then we gradually gain some idea of what it was that people vividly connected with the word "body" in those days. Namely two things.

First and foremost they took the body seriously. They thought its every detail terribly important and they took it literally. They accepted it in a way which we are no longer capable of today. Even the comparison of the church building with the Lord's body would have been unthinkable without this absolute earnestness about the body's structure. The human form was for them a representation of absolute form. The body had not grown together out of a series of accidents but had been given by the Creator in accordance with the sacred plan. To them this real body of everyday reality in its everyday structure was created "in the image of God." In it, God had imparted his own form, first on the sixth day of the creation, as Genesis described it, and then once more when the word became flesh. In the Savior, in his holy body and in that which visibly befell him and in what he did, the first revelation was clarified, surmounted and founded anew. And ever since then all true growth and all sacred life had imitated this revelation which had happened in form and in history—for in the body of the Lord the eternal had become visible. The Middle Ages certainly did not simply imagine their conception of the body. To be sure, much of their knowledge was superficial. What lay inside the body could only be guessed at: anatomy was unknown since it was thought that even cutting into the structure of the dead body was forbidden to men. This led to lacks in the teachings and in the work, for many of these conjectures were utterly false. But even the renunciation of anatomy and of the living model prove how serious a matter the real body was to these people and with what great awe they experienced the sacred connection between its structure and the holy chastity of its life.

But—this is the second thing—the body which was seen with such realism was not a rigid pattern. The very nature of its appearance which they took so seriously was the fundamental articulation for the wealth of forms in a free and radiant life. Body was both given and ever effected anew. The body could transform itself, it was overflowing with possibilities, it could shine, it could grow tall and unspeakably glorious; and the body could also go to ruin. The body could fulfill everything and transform everything. Body was bound to no definite size and to no definite form and yet it possessed an eternal structure; it could assume this form and later on another and yet through all this remain true to itself. Body was a work to be continually accomplished between God and the Soul, ever new interpretation into living freedom. Even the fact that the saints were often hard on it did not at bottom mean a mortification of the body but rather its sacred interpretation. Had the body not meant anything to them they would not have treated it as they did.

These, then, are the approximate premises for the assertion that the congregation or the church building itself are the mighty holy body of the Lord. He who says this believes that the Lord's body is so rich that it can assume all these forms. And at the same time he believes that the body's structure is the form of the eternal, so that wherever the eternal takes on body this articulation becomes visible. The great churches and cathedrals are for him a whole cosmos, a revelation of eternal structure, objective form set before God.

Personally we believe that the sacred objectivity of these old concepts is true and that we will ourselves have to be converted to it. The times have erred far away from it. Sacred structure is no longer understood as that which it actually is: as structure, as the dogmatics of eternity. Rather is it understood in the same way in which historical painting understands history. Idle folk run about within it and seek out their own private viewpoints, have their private pleasures and write them down in private books. Even photography was invented at the right moment for them, for by means of it reality can be deprived of all form and can be misinterpreted in every way; and at all events it put the movable standpoint in the place of the gloriously objective structural plan. Assuredly the medieval master who taught that "the beautiful is that which is pleasing to see" seemed to acknowledge them to be right. But what a lot of misunderstandings! How distorted the meaning of each of these few words! That old "beauty" was the final witness to the truth, the "laughter of the universe" which simply became itself, child in the Father's hand. And "to please," "*placet*" was the "yes" of the creature, its final, consummate consent; "seeing" was acceptance and response through a believing pair of eyes.

But the total con-version and re-version of the building art must come to pass wholly out of what is genuine.

We cannot return to the early cathedrals and take up their interrupted discipline once more. This was the error of the Historicists. Even the tools, our "technology," would fail us. It would of course be possible to copy the deep doorways and the mighty pillars of the Romanesque or the pointed arches of the Gothic. But it would not be true. For us the wall is no longer heavy masonry but rather a taut membrane, we know the great tensile strength of steel and with it we have conquered the vault. For us the building materials are something different from what they were to the old masters. We know their inner structure, the positions of their atoms, the course of their inner tensions. And we build in the knowledge of all this—it is irrevocable. The old, heavy forms would turn into theatrical trappings in our hands and the people would see that they were an empty wrapping. They would draw premature conclusions about the matter which is served by these empty forms.

But in a far profounder sense we cannot return to the Middle Ages. The great realities of the cathedral are no longer real to us. This does not mean that "in themselves" they are no longer true. No, they are as true to us as on their first day and they move us deeply. What a "spire" is and proclaims, the procession of "pillars" and "arches," the crowd of "pinnacles" and "responders"—these are valid for all times, as valid as a painting by Lochner or the sculptures of Bamberg. But even so we can no longer build these things because life has gone on and the reality which is our task and which is given into our hands possesses completely different, perhaps poorer, form. Deep in our hearts we know what the solemn words of the old cathedrals mean, and still it is not given to us to realize them as that which they once were. We know what a Gothic spire was but our own spire is something very different. For us the old words no longer name the same living reality. Here we are not speaking as historians or theorists whose only question is "how it actually was at that time," regardless of whether or not that past reality can still be brought into living consummation today. We speak rather as creating men, as masters of building who are supposed to make out, not with what may be theoretically "right," but rather with what is at hand, with what is real, here and now. There is a great difference between an ab-

stract truth and an architectural reality. For the master builder, what proves
true is true, real what realizes. In his bare workshop the things are worth
only as much as they can perform. When he perseveres in the genuine he
does what God wants of him, even if this genuine thing be poor. We should
not fall upon his work and demand realizations of theoretical truths which
he cannot provide, for then nonentities may arise, unproved fabrications
and faithless sacrality—and along with these weeds the people may throw
away the seed out of which the genuine might grow. It is easy to say that we
can no longer build in the medieval manner and yet it is difficult to hold out
where we are, to make out with what is given us and to avoid that historistical
doing which uses only the historical things and not the historical forms.

On the other hand it does not suffice to work honestly with the means and
forms of our own time. It is only out of sacred reality that sacred building
can grow. What begets sacred works is not the life of the world but the life
of faith—the faith, however, of our own time. This is the third thing: that
sacred substance out of which churches can be built must be alive and real
to us. It would be so simple to go back to the old teaching and to say that we
should build the "body of Christ"—it would even be modern. Today people
again recall the old terms and like to use them. They speak of the body of
the Lord and relate the word to the individual, to the community and even
to the works of their hands. Or they say that man was created in the "image
of God," and once again they call the church service "God's work." The old
words awaken in them memories and hopes. But people no longer combine
any clear conceptions with them; they use them in Latin, solemnly, like ancient conceits of a holy theology but they do not use them to name something which they see in each detail of outline, form and color. At the time
when these words were discovered they named straightforwardly that which
was seen and experienced; but when we repeat them today we express at
best a feeling. Nowadays we no longer see the body as people formerly saw
it, with luminous head, tall, radiant and buoyant. Our body is inert and
heavy, bound to the spot. And so it is that when we speak of the sacred body
our only possibility is to think either completely honestly of this our body

as we see it, exercise it, heal it every day, as our science has investigated it, as it now is—admittedly a needy premise for theology—or to think of something generally solemn. He who calls the church a "work of God" either means precisely what is meant today by the word "work," or he means something completely vague, which means that he doesn't think at all but only has feelings. The old words named a very definite and particular sight. And since we today are no longer capable of seeing this sight at all, we have found a strange way out: the sacred is invisible and the old words referred to miracles. Historicism exists in the realm of the sacred, too, and it has little prospect of standing the test of time.

This, then is our task:

To build churches out of that reality which we experience and verify every day; to take this our own reality so seriously and to recognize it to be so holy that it may be able to enter in before God. To renew the old teachings concerning sacred work by trying to recognize the body, even as it is real to us today, as creature and as revelation, and by trying to render it so; to reinstitute the body in its dignity and to do our work so well that this body may prove to be "sacred body." And beyond all this to guard ourselves against repeating the old words when for us no living content is connected with them.

In the following we will attempt to show, in the two examples of the eye and the hand, that it is possible to believe in the body as we know it today as a creature; then we will attempt to show that our work as we practice it today is good and that it could well be made into "God's work." And finally we shall try to show in what respects this work must be differentiated from our daily work.

The Eye

How beautiful is our knowledge of the human eye! How it waits to be rightly understood! As eye, the body sees the light which is in the world. The light comes to it over the things but goes forth from the stars.

"Star"—that is primary streaming light. Three things make up its form:

the generating center: a shining point

the rays of light: the paths which go out from the center in all directions

the sphere of light: the growing ball to which the center expands.

These three elements together make up the star-form. Each one of them is the expression and the transformation of the others and each is unthinkable without them—the form is wholly unified. Center expands into sphere, rays spring from the center point and beget the surrounding ball. He who names one part names the whole. The star is primary form.

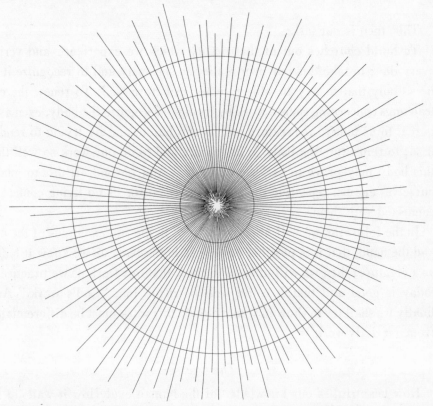

The light beats a path through the space, irradiates it and takes it up into the star-image. At last the light strikes a thing and then this thing in turn

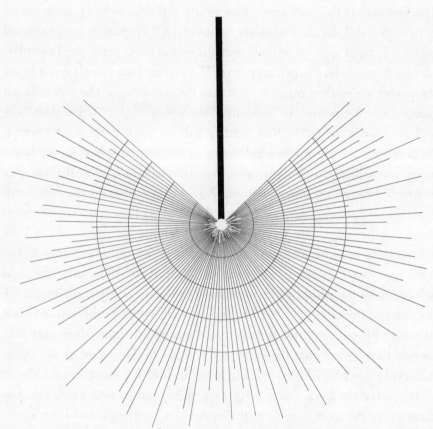

begins to shine. Since, however, the light and the star are one and the same,
it is in reality the star which reaches this thing on the rays of light and which
is united with it. In the course of this process the shining object takes a part
of the light, now changed to darkness, into itself. The rest it passes on and
in so doing the thing itself becomes a star. At each point on its shining
surface the star-form is formed once again and colored light streams out in
all directions.

But these countless new stars on the radiant thing have no independent
existence. Their sphere of light exists only as long as they continue to be
fed from the primary light. Hanging from it by the bridge of rays, they
"de-pend" upon it.

The first star is the only one which really unfolds, welling forth out of its own center. All the later ones are "open stars." They, too, are composed of center, rays and sphere but their center does not itself generate. Inwardly, the center depends on the primary star. The primary star sends out a beam to this center which then transforms it into the star-image. The center is not source but turning-point—it "mediates" the primal light. "Open stars" denote those places where the first light founds its settlements in the world.

Such open stars are made whole only in the primary star, for it is the primary star which closes their openness. They stand open to it through a "window," through an inner opening. Nor do they pass on the full light. Their light is "broken," for one part of the original light, now transformed to darkness, has sunk into the depths of the things. The strained-out light which remains goes on as color. Therefore it is not quite accurate to say that the essence of the things finds expression in their color, since the light which passes to the inside and is consumed there is exactly complementary to the color of the object. Indeed the light which passes to the inside is just what would fill out the color to make up the original light. More correctly we would have to say that the color is the reply to the inside of the thing, and as reply it is also of course a key to the inside. We recognize the things in their colored shadows. Color is light which has united with an object. The surface of the things is clothed with "open stars"—open toward the sun— or with "open sockets," and in this latter connection it makes sense to say that the things of the world are covered with eyes.

When his eye sees, the human being becomes open for the light. It enters through a window. Once inside, it comes together at the focal point, whence it shines, again a star, onto the horizon of the retina. Thus the star-image comes into being for a third time in the eye.

The light comes as a ray from the outside to the star in the eye, too, and this second star is "open" in the direction of the bridge of rays. If the eye closes, the star is extinguished. The star in the eye lasts only as long as it hangs, through the window, on the seen thing. Therefore the star in the eye is not a rebirth of the thing in the world but only its subordinate dwelling.

This object reaches into the eye over the bridge of rays. Actually, of course, it is not the object which enters the eye, for the object itself is in turn dependent on the primary star—the object's sphere of light exists only as long as it "de-pends" on the original light. Thus a chain of connections develops, the first light is passed on again and again and each time it produces a star. The eye is complete only in the sun, and so actually we see nothing except the sun and the things as shadows in it.

Even of the colorful surface of the world we see only the side turned toward us, and this, too, we see in an apparent coherence which does not exist at all "in reality." The eye cannot see the backs of the things, their depths and furrows, the things which are disguised or turned away from it. The eye is easily deceived and easily led astray and therefore it has often been accused of being a poor instrument. Extensive theories have been built up about the "optical illusion," but these theories are in themselves an optical illusion since they are deluded as to the eye and its meaning. The eye is not an apparatus for the purpose of recognizing the things. Rather is it man's profound and open answer to streaming light. The eye sees the star without illusion and in the star it can see the things, but only insofar as they themselves are star. In them it recognizes the star-image, nothing more, for in the star everything is arching smoothness without furrows or depths. The eye alters the world according to the plan of the star, and the eye itself is built according to this plan, in order that the world may enter into it. When we look at the world it becomes a star to which the eye replies—an open star in which one segment is lacking, an open star which is made whole in the sun.

This is approximately what we know today about seeing. It was not known formerly and it is glorious. Only one thing is lacking here: that warm and good understanding which finds meaning and form in all these things.

Does not to behold something mean to choose one particular thing out of the world and to move it into the center of the eye? Does it not mean to place this chosen thing as the only sun in a new universe, to make oneself, one's own body, into the sphere of this shining thing? To form one's own body into a dark world arching about the new central sun of the seen thing? Does it not mean to establish across and beyond this thing a relationship with the primal star, to make oneself "dependent" upon it, to nourish oneself from it and to unite oneself with it?

And all this has a form.

The eye is form, beautifully and wisely built in accordance with the design of the star-image. It is the answering body which sees the light and is inwardly enriched by it. Thus this is the way the body looks when it gives answer to the stars; the body's meeting with the light "looks like" this.

The open eye is a valid image of the body and hence of the human being; its open shell-like form is a genuine symbol. This sign stands for the human being and we may designate the human being with it since we did not invent it: the body itself created this form. We can learn from this primal sign that the body is built on encounter, that it is answer to light, that the human being is an "open form"; that we recognize the world only as shadow in the light and that we never possess it completely; and that consequently the human being is not a microcosmos but rather a deficient being, needful of completion. Or far more, that by making himself into an open form, thus repeating inwardly the openness of the universe and its dependence on light, the human being may renew within himself the structure of the world.

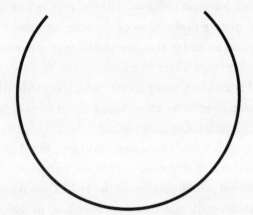

Only that eye which could look at the world on all sides and which could surround the world on the outside with its own horizon would see the world completely. And only those things, which stars are, are complete. The world disposes itself around them as perfect eye. But the horizon of the retina remains open, the human being clings to the distant light—and the constellation of the things are open, too.

The eye, then, is not a star, as is so often said, but rather answer to it. It is circumference, dark, hollow and in readiness. But the star is center which gives itself forth in shining radiance. Eye and star hold dialogues, their forms complete one another. Here we see that there are certain forms which are based on one another—forms which find their meaning only when they meet, forms which become whole in each other. And we see that the forms of the living body are significant because they have meaning in discourse and dialogue.

Whether the eye is capable of action?
Our language thinks so, for it speaks of "casting" a glance, of shining eyes, and it says that we see the things, whereas to be optically correct we would have to say that the things look at us. Our feelings think so too, for they know that the things are changed by the way our eyes rest upon them, that the things can become little and grey, even evil, or that they can rise up to smile at us, that they can grow and radiate under our glance. Our feelings know that eyes can enchant or encourage, command or obliterate. The eye can make the things so trusting that they advance to meet us. Obviously all this means more than simply the outward ability to avoid a meeting, to cast down the eyes, to close them; more, too, than the ability to turn the eyes in a particular direction and to focus them at a particular distance. Actually all this says that through our eyes we may yield ourselves.

Here our present knowledge helps us no farther, the question has not been investigated. But it seems to us that a dark counter-current must be assumed which flows toward the things when we look at them, a sort of influence in which inner being is communicated to the being of the things. For clearly the creatures on which our eyes rest are addressed in their very depths, are comprehended and changed. Everything which is asserted and believed about the effects of seeing concerns the whole, never the details; it is as if a dark power, utterly without contour, streamed out through the eye. This meeting would be consummated in all purity where one pair of eyes looks deep into another, where darkness enters into darkness and where, from being to being, purest concord happens. Perhaps the figure of the seeing eye could be read backward: then the nerves would be the channels of the dark current which enters space at the retina. In the act of seeing the things, the light current from the outside and the dark from the inside would unite and together they would create the "image."

The Hand

How beautiful is the hand! How much it can do and how beautiful its function!

The hand can radiate.

The arm rises, the fist clenches and over the single pointing finger the gathered power discharges—the hand becomes radiating point. But when it opens, stretching all fingers outward from the palm, it is an open star at the end of the arm.

The hand can hollow itself.

The fingers come together to form a bowl, empty and open in the movement of holding. In the cupping motion the two hands come together to make up one single bowl.

The hand which we offer is both "active" star-image and receptive, empty form.

The hand can touch.

The farthest finger-tip softly touches a thing, the gentlest power of communication flows out to it and slowly, softly it reveals itself.

With the first gentle touch the reaching movement is reversed: surrender to the thing becomes submersion in it. Quietly the hand rests on the thing and fingers it. The hand can reassure, love and bless. Here being surrenders to being. Here is healing. What happens in the laying-on of hands may be compared to the communication of intrinsic being which occurs when the eyes rest on a thing. Both eye and hand work changes deep within. The mysterious meeting of one pair of eyes in another corresponds lastly with the clasping of two hands whose streams of being are exchanged and become one. (And the eye also possesses that second movement of folding one's own hands: it is the movement of closing the lids.)

The hand can feel.

The hand which yields itself to a thing assumes the form of the thing. Yet it does this in such a way that where the thing protrudes the hand is concave and where the thing is concave the hand is pliable. Thus the hand is "answer" to the formed-ness of the things and in this it is like the eye which sees. The hand runs over the surface provingly and this movement is at once feeling and communicating, moulding and a calm stroking, a sort of silent conversing.

In many ways the hand understands the world better than the eye. It "sees" the world from all sides. The hand can grasp. Its fingers close around the thing, forming a vault. The power of the hand to radiate streams back into itself and in a dark current this power flows about the clasped thing, awakening the answer within it. Thus the thing is taken up completely into the circulation of the body; it is buried in the hollow of the hand: the hand can conceal—and this the eye cannot do either, since for it the world is always open. The hand can take a piece of the world completely into itself and contain it wholly; it can grasp the thing from all sides. The hand makes an entire world, it notices the backs of the things, too, the indentations, the dissimulations. But the hand's world is not large—it cannot reach very far and its capacity is small. The hand is built for what is nearby, for the limited, for the things themselves while the eye is in reality built for the sun.

Eye and hand are sister and brother for both apprehend the surfaces— that is, the ex-pressions of the things, the utterances through which they speak. But where the hand itself possesses depth and inner structure it opens up for itself a part of the world which is closed to the eye: the inner space of the things. With a testing push or pull it explores the mass. The "grasp-

ing" hand strains the material until it begins to grow soft. The resistance
of the mass is expressed in the increasing tension of sinews and muscles, in
the growing pressure within the bony structure. The hand creates an answer
to the insides of the things within its own inner structure; and with the same
instrument it can form them and also weigh them.

If we want to test the weight of a thing we must lift it, hold it suspended
against the force of gravity. This happens through the hand. The hand
passes its inner stress on into the arm which in turn passes this stress into
the body. Hidden within the body is a system of tension running over sinews,
muscles and bones, through arm, spine and legs, from the weighted object
down to the earth. A sort of pathway is formed between the earth and the
thing, a course which passes over the body as the bearing bridge. Thus we
may say that as the seeing eye is related to the sun high overhead, so is the
grasping, weighing hand related to the depths of the earth.

It is not by becoming mass itself but rather by translating mass into
buoyance that the body perceives the inner nature of the world, its dull,
massive heaviness. Body which apprehends the heavy things is not weight
but response to weight. Its answer to the heavy compactness of the world's
matter reads "column" and "cable." Mass is expanding, unformed, roomy;
the body's answer is linear, slender, articulate. Mass is fullness. The body
replies with the "skeleton," a delicate fabric of curves in space. Therefore
it is false to accuse the body of being earth-bound or to contrast it with the
supposed lightness of some "spiritual" principle. By its very nature, the
body brings into its encounter with the heavy earth the will to transform
dull massiveness into buoyant power. The body is not primarily weight, but
lightness—"power" which interlaces space on linear paths.

We experience mass in the growing tension of ligaments, which is to say
that we experience it lineally. This very simple circumstance reveals its
relationship to numbers and to the lineal law of their growth which we find
expressed in the curve. The experience of mass can be "reckoned," it can be
delineated in the movement of numbers, it can be represented in curves.
During the last few centuries this fact has largely determined our picture

of the world and also our work itself. The experience of what lies within
the things came late and when it came it was overwhelming. For a long
time hardly anything else counted. Afterward the "grasping" hand was
bitterly attacked—the hand which saw only the massiveness and weight in
the things and which discovered in them only their function. And when, at
last, the eye and the "world of forms" were given their rightful place beside
the grasping hand—and with them the outlines of the things, their shapes
and colors and the timbre which is in the world—all this was felt to be a
liberation.

We do not contradict this. By itself the hand obviously provides a contribution to the recognition of the real world—but again, only as an organ
for the depths of the world's matter. If this aspect remains isolated, the
image of the world is distorted and the work even more. But we may not now
replace the "haptics" of the grasping hand with the "optics" of the seeing
eye lest a new distortion arise. The liberation must lead from the part to the
whole, it must place the eye, the ear, the whole body, next to the hand so
that once again we may achieve total works and so that the world may become
whole once more. The hand itself must become whole again, too, "feeling"
must enter in next to "grasping," the hand must once more become "eye,—
and like the eye it must come to stand for the whole body since like the eye
the hand, too, is a little human being, is the image, the body of man.
("Manu" means "little man.") Within this whole, however, a very high
place is owed to the "concept," to the "grasping" hand. It is not true that
concepts understand nothing of the essence of the things. The concept answers a particular part of the world through a wonderful fabric of curves.
Here it achieves profoundest concord with the world. The concept and its
work are lofty deeds of the mind.

We could continue to consider the body in this way; the image would
grow ever richer but in essence it would remain the same. We found the
body in ever changing form: as hollow ball in relation to light, as linear
scaffold in relation to weight, as ray, star, surface, arch. And we found that

the body is not ultimately bound to any form at all but is extraordinarily free. The world is filled with a great dialogue which passes back and forth between thing and thing, between form and form. The body is drawn into this great flow of speech. It is open to every invocation which comes to it from the forms and it replies to them with clear forms of its own, forms which it assumes for the moment and then relinquishes once more. This dialogue is not limited to the sound of words alone: it is exercised with the whole body and all its limbs. Thus the body is constantly formed and yet, beyond all transformation, it remains true to itself. If we observe only its material—which is now eye, now hand, now foot, now ray, now ball, then bowl, then ligament, then shaft—this material seems to be hardly more than a plastic mass out of which that something which imparts the answer kneads its forms of reply. If this "something" is the "soul" then the body is hardly more than its changing image, its message into the world—and also the soul is wedded to the body far more intimately than was previously supposed. But if it is the body which imparts one answer after the other, which gives one invocation after the other—and we are very inclined to this opinion—then the body is "really" something, and this something commands the material almost like a sovereign, playing with the forms and yet not losing itself in them. Then body also means faithfulness to one's own form; then it is not something-or-other, not some proteus-like fluid, but rather clear structure to which everything applies which we mean when we speak of "form." The body is consumed utterly in its momentary form and takes this form completely literally. However it is not ultimately bound to this form. Rather is it prepared to answer all sorts of situations in the manner appropriate to the moment through forms which are ever different and ever clear, and yet beyond them all it remains itself. And so the body would be both potentiality and form: potentiality, which can take on almost all forms, and form, which, as it is, is serious and complete.

What we have said may not be exact in every detail. It is neither our task nor our field to provide an anthropological doctrine. Our concern is rather good guidance to true work. And since our work can be true work only if it grows out of what is real, we wanted to show that reality is not such a bad building material after all and that we could make out with it without fleeing into historisticism. What we have pointed out is not actually new. Children learn it in school. But we believe that it might be looked at for once as if it *were* new, as if we had just heard about it for the first time. We believe that we can accept reality understandingly, as being made up of things and processes which exist and which have a form whose meaning is reasonable and deductible—as things and processes whose form and meaning coincide. It must be possible for us to trust the body to be what it "looks like." And it must be possible to trust that the Creator meant something in giving it this form and no other.

Perhaps in this way we would arrive sooner at a comprehensible teaching about man, which indeed we all need so badly. It seems to us that at the present time no tremendous outlay of ceremonious metaphysics would be necessary in order to get to the root of what man actually is, and it seems to us, too, that no such difficult books need be written about it—books whose readers even at the end have still not found out how many legs are allotted to a man. Perhaps it would be better to look for once in awe at what is there, not with great learnedness but with the warm understanding of the good mother. She knows that it is the details which are the really important things about her little boy and she tends to base the proof for the divine origin of man on the fact that this little boy happens to be just as he is, with two feet, on each of them five toes; and she is convinced that she will one day be held accountable for having kept his ears clean, since she believes that these precise ears are a part of the particular revelation given in this little creature. But the philosophical mother, to whom these ears are not "of the essence" has little prospect of eternal life.

Would not this perhaps be even the more correct way of learning to see revelation in the body, too, and of learning to believe once more in the sacred body? A body ever effected as speech and answer would not be difficult to believe in as an image or a likeness or as an answer to the Creator's invocation. And it would be understandable that the body can become unutterably beautiful when it makes itself wholly into a loving answer under the eyes of God. The body constantly enacted or effected would be the most serious of tasks. And lastly it would even be more comprehensible to us that the body, giving answer anew to the voice of the Creator, can be restored in regenerate form. If it is true that man is something constantly effected, constantly regenerated, if it is true that he is a creature who ever "de-pends" on his Creator, a creature who is capable of hearing and of answering God's holy word and work, then he really is a likeness, and then God himself is not something-or-other but rather has a form, a form which is shown in man, not directly, but as that reply to God's own form which has been awakened in earthly matter.

Painting

How beautiful are the works of the creating body and how gloriously they reveal its innermost being!

When a painter paints his picture almost the same thing happens in the open as that which takes place in secret when the eye sees. It is not, as the ancient philosophers thought, and as has been repeated ever since, that this painter has a little picture in his head which he reproduces by covering a canvas with forms and colors, continually testing to see whether or not he has copied it exactly. It is rather that in the beginning he has only a seed within himself, and he takes care not to think this seed out into an "inner picture" (which he could easily do in every detail) because then he would do his own work ahead of time and afterward he would succeed only in making a tired reproduction—should he still have any desire to make the boring transcription. Far more does his picture grow under his hand as a young creature, and his eye, astonished and moved, reports to the inside what is taking place there on the outside. From time to time, then, the painter steps back and views the work with an appraising eye. The eye itself cannot actually paint. It is conceivable that it could. The motion picture projector gives an example of how a light can be shone through an exposed ground, which has been fixed and made transparent, so that the negative appears positive. Otherwise, however, this occurs as simple reflection and without any creative ingredient. This the eye cannot do. It can see pictures but it cannot produce them. Its radiance is dark and without outline. Therefore in painting the eye weds itself with the hand which is color-blind. And hence what arises is not radiation (projection) but a giving forth, a birth (production). The eye rests encouragingly on the hand and what comes into being is neither a reflection of the world nor a reflection of what lies within, rather it is image. But now the spot where the image grows is not the inner retina but the external canvas. In painting it is almost as if the painter were to transpose his retina to the outside, as if he thus made the image objective and public and placed it where the visible world stood before.

Sculpture

Sculpture, too, is a work of the hands. The hand lays hold of a material and models out of it the image. The hand awakens it to speech. Flattening, testing and improving it moves over the surface and the eye watches, resting quietly on the busy hand. Here again the eye's contribution is purely feminine.

But sculpture is primarily the work of the feeling hand, not of the grasping hand. The sculptural form has its own true place on the surface: it is imposed form. What lies beneath should carry and support this form, and when really successful, it expresses itself through the surface.

Here there are two borderline cases. One case is where the sculptor chooses a material because it possesses the baser quality of sticking together and of occupying space—here he can impose a form onto it, a form in which the material itself participates only inasfar as it holds the shape and prevents it from immediately dissolving. This is the case of pure minting. A pure form is pressed onto an impressionable material. Wax and soft clay are worked in this way. And this is also the case with casting: a liquid material is poured into a hollow form in which it hardens.

The other borderline case—here the sculptor literally carves out his image—is where the sculptor wins the form from his material. He lets the grain of the wood or the vein in a block of marble "speak," too. But this "speaking" is not real dialogue since the material does not understand the form which it should have but only contributes its accidental physical qualities or at most the form of its growth. Only dumbly does the stuff sense what is imposed upon it. In no case does the material take a greater part than this in sculptural work. It is dangerous to compare the educator or the politician to the sculptor, for the latter imposes his form on a dumb material.

In sculpture the hand reverses itself, as it were: its particular way of feeling becomes assertion. The hand which perceives a thing by feeling fingers the outside of it, thus noticing its external form, and through this form the hand can guess at what lies within. In a sculptural work, this act of feeling becomes utterance. The hand turns into a speaking form and places itself on the outside as a work. Thus this work's strange existence between the dimensions is explained. This work is spatial but its spatiality is that of an oft bent surface—and there is something else too, for this surface is given depth by the quiet submission of the sculptural mass. The way in which the depths of the sculpture participate here corresponds to the silent communication of the hand which rests softly on a thing. One is transposed into the other, the sculptor exchanges the world for his own hand, he puts his hand in the place of a thing in the world.

Building

The art of building is not a genuine work of the hand since it is done with the whole body. The laborers lift up the materials, place them one on top of the other and join them together. They execute movements which correspond to the forms of the growing part of the building and they deposit these movements in the building materials. In this way the act of raising turns to upright structure. The workers go over the wall with the trowel, and out of their stroking motion comes a skin of color or plaster. They saw and plane the wood, draw and forge the iron. Each limb of the body moves in its own particular way and all of them together create the building as a second body.

Nor is building the work of one man. Under the head foreman a whole ordered company of men takes part in the work on the building.

What then comes into being is first and foremost circumscribed space—shelter, living space, ceremonial space, a space which replaces the space of the world. We could almost say, and indeed it is true, that building is based on the inner spaciousness of the body, on the knowledge of its extent and the form of its growth, on the knowledge of its articulation and of its power to expand. Indeed it is with the body that we experience building, with the outstretched arms and the pacing feet, with the roving glance and with the ear, and above all else in breathing. Space is dancingly experienced. But the surroundings are the inversion of the dance: that space inside of which the dance extends itself, that space which stands ready for the body, is not, as is usually assumed, the outward radiating of the body but rather its inverted space—the body's space turned inside out and projected into the outer world. The body's space, however, forces itself outward whereas the space of the building forces itself inward so that its "skin" lies close to that of the dancing people. The "inside" of the structure overflows, the content of the space is larger than its "skin."

Shell Construction

At its outer limit the building space is bordered by the walls. Here difficulties arise because this all-embracing construction has itself two sides, one turned toward the world, the other toward the inner space; and between them is again a mass, and this mass is itself a particular "work-body"; and, again, seen from the outside, the whole structure is sculpture. Thus the layers and processes of work interweave in many varied ways. It would be quite simple if the entire enclosing construction were only a membrane which spanned the space of the inner form. This is the case in the stereometrical body where the surface is the exact expression of the contents: in a

ball, which has the greatest content in respect to space, the smallest expanse
in respect to surface, and in which surface and content correspond exactly
to each other, both signifying the same thing, each in its own way. If truth-
fulness consists in clear expression, then shell construction is the truest of
all ways of building for the shell adheres completely to the inner space, and
it seems—none of these things can be proved—that the inner condition
within such a shell, the static articulation of its stuff, is "contained without
a remainder" in this "equation." When, in addition, the form of the people's
ordering corresponds with the spatial form, we achieve a completely "unani-
mous" work in which the whole structure is permeated from the inside to the
outside by the same form. Here would be realized that total architecture
which is the dream of our new building art.

Building as Sculpture

We can also build in a completely different way.

Walls and construction may be regarded as a plastic theme and we may
then allow space and walls to orchestrate the structure contrapuntally. Then,
like the material of a statue, that which happens within the walls themselves
participates only softly through their "skin." The construction contributes
little to the form—its task is hardly more than to provide a stiffening for it.
The most magnificent example of this type of building is provided by the
human body itself. The body hides the skeleton and the play of muscles, it
reveals them only by intimation, making them as it were into the theme of a
sculptural composition which plays freely and in many variations about
what lies within. The Greeks built in this manner. Their building is not a
form effecting the conquest of gravity as is the Gothic—rather do gravity
and its conquest here become one single artistic theme. This form speaks in
the Doric as it may speak in a statue. It would be senseless to call this sort
of building untrue. It is conceived differently from the skeletal structure
but in its own way it is honest. Even now it is not obsolete. In our own time

we have an utterly new and genuine relationship to the block, to delicate and organic contour, to the succulent abundance of Doric capitals, to the melody of Ionic fluting. In the buildings of antiquity the space is obviously little more than that which plays round the contours of the sculpture, gathering itself in the hollows to run off in the fluting of the columns. It is significant that many of our own very beautiful new buildings of the sculptural type— for instance those of Mies—have almost no outer walls and are only "of necessity" closed by means of glass panes. In a higher sense they remain open.

Skeletal Construction

Skeletal construction, the third way of building, comes from still another source.

This type of construction springs from a concept of the world in which matter gathers itself to a skeleton of slender arches of tension—a concept of the world which sees space shot through with powers. ("Dynamism" is a false name for this since the ancient δυναμις is dark and compact like a Doric capital.) This method of building is of recent origin—unless one believes it to have been prefigured in the wooden halls of our forefathers which disappeared long ago. This type of construction found its first great representation in the Gothic and it is consummated in our "technology." To be sure, the Gothic skeleton knows of practically no wrought members. It is limited to groups of slender, resistant columns and consequently it remains vaulting and upright structure—but as such it is formed completely of buoyancy. "Technology" brings for the first time the tensile strength of steel and with it the play of upright and cable. Seen from the vantage point of "technology" the Gothic method is antiquated. But "technology" had the misfortune not to be taken seriously and accusations have been made against it similar to those made against the grasping hand. It was born into a small-minded age.

Tent Construction

Actually the skeletal type of construction is spaceless also. For it, space is only the abstract means of orienting a curve, that something through which its powers pass. If we wish to win a living-space from this scaffold, we must span it. (This is obviously only an act of "self-defense" for the play of these interlacing members is at its most expressive when it weaves through free space, unspanned and uninhabitable, as in the tracery of a Gothic spire.)

Actually, where skeletal construction is used to provide living space, we must speak of tent construction. This is the form of transition to shell construction. And it would seem that we are now undergoing this transformation in our own time.

When, in skeletal construction, that power of the body which answers gravity is turned into a work, it can be compared to the hand which closes about a thing. Here, as in the hand, lines of force encircle the hidden content. Man has laid his own hand about himself as the content. It is immaterial whether the building art occurs as shell form, as sculpture, as skeletal or tent construction, for each time it is the "body" which turns about, which moves to the outside and which makes itself into its own shelter. That which made the body as the first answer given to the world, builds for it the house of architecture.

Thus the works of art would be closely related to the body which creates them. Not that they are "enlarged body"—this they are not. We receive them into ourselves with the body and this may have led us to mistake them for amplifications of the body, since the theories often confuse the means of perception with the work itself. Rather do they stand in an active reciprocal relation to the body, but again not within the simple dialogue of question and answer. The eye is hollow and dark, the light is shining abundance: eye and light converse. A painting, however, is colored "image" just as much as the image on the retina, except that it lies outside of the body and can be looked at as if it were a colored world. Sculpture is like the palm of the hand, but one can put one's hand upon it. Works are "other body." That something which addresses the world and replies to the world in the changing forms of the body here exchanges that which originally confronted it as world for something second in which the encounter is consummated. That which happens buried deep within the body is created here outside of it. Then body can live in its work, work can become the body's house. These two are sibling forms.

All these things are thoughts which occurred to us about our own work and much may be wrong or even false in them. It is neither our task nor our intention to invent a science of the arts—we trust the scholars will take care of that—and for the things which are going to be said in this book it is not necessary that our suppositions be perfect. The book stands on its own feet: we have not wished to set forth a theory and we shall not now proceed to a practical application. It is too bad that these things are always discussed scientifically—that is to say starting from observations and ending in definitions—and that they are never discussed for the architect, that is to say starting from creation and aiming at right doing and true works. And so, may these thoughts have the good quality that their goal is the doctrine of work—and we have found that they do help us onward. If they do prove true, then the works themselves are closely related to the body and almost all the things can be said about them which were said about the body: that they are an inexhaustible task, that they may turn out to be great or lowly, that there are whole hierarchies of works.

There are levels of doing. At the highest step in this order stands that work in which man spends himself utterly in order to consummate the world as sacred likeness. This work awakens the slumbering image and makes whole the creaturehood of the world. If you wish, this is the worship, the service of God, not service to the Godhead in becoming, as Scheler erred so terribly, but service to the image in becoming. The creative hand yields itself completely into the hand of God the Creator and God's guiding hand is

placed upon it. God sees his world through the knowing eyes of his creatures. God lifts the heavy things which we lift, he places his two hands
easingly under ours. Such work is holy work, blessed with an abundance
of fruit—it is, if we wish, sacrament.

One thing it is not: it is not prayer. Work, even work in its noblest magnificence, is service to the world in whose fundament the sacred image rests.
Prayer, however, is the clear, pure invocation of God. The man who prays
does not busy himself with the things, he leaves them. He turns his eyes to
God, opens his arms and hands and empties them before the Lord. Or he
folds them and confesses his helplessness, he ties them and shows that their
work is over. By this he does not mean to say that he has freed himself from
the things, for this he cannot do nor may he attempt it. It is out of his eyes
that the creature looks to the Lord and it is in his hands that the creature
grows empty. Man takes God's creatures with him into his prayer. The
mother, who has served God in her own holy way by the bearing and rearing
of her children, places them beside her and puts both arms about them as
she prays. With them she enters in before God. In the same way everyone
brings that which is entrusted to him in love, opened, to the Lord and gives
it back to him. In prayer the things are reversed—their pyramid whose summit was man turns into an empty form at whose very bottom the open human
being stands.

Creation begins when God calls on man and names him. Man answers
with his existence, his body, his work, and God blesses these things. But
prayer begins when man calls out to God and awaits an answer. Worldly
work is God's work with the world, praying work is the world's work with
God, at first a work of helplessness and afterward a work rewarded by God.
It is foolhardy to say that man should make God into his answer or that man
should bring him forth, and it is sacrilege when it means that God lies within
man's power. But it becomes true when it is taken up into God's loving freedom: in his love it is his habit to answer his creature. He gives himself into
his creature's hands and heart and his creature may move him.

PART II
The First Six Plans

Sacred Inwardness
The Ring

FOR THE CELEBRATION of the Lord's supper a moderately large, well-proportioned room is needed, in its center a table and on the table a bowl of bread and a cup of wine. The table may be decorated with candles and surrounded by seats for the congregation.

That is all. Table, space and walls make up the simplest church.

The table is the sustaining earth which rises up for the solemn celebration.

The cup is the innermost casing about the secret, its first form. As such, it is also the prototype of the people surrounding the table and of the walls surrounding the people—and thus it is, as it were, an innermost church.

The candle is living light streaming out of the center.

The space is sacred abundance.

Walls and roof are the final outermost covering.

The little congregation sits or stands about the table. The Lord is in the center as he promised to be when he said that wherever a few should gather in his name he would be in the midst of them.

There have been greater forms of church building than this one but this is not the right time for them. We cannot continue on from where the last cathedrals left off. Instead we must enter into the simple things at the source of the Christian life. We must begin anew and our new beginning must be genuine. The small congregation is given us today, the "coming together of two or three," the communion of the table, and certainly for us the Lord is in the midst of men.

Even when a new church is to be built, the simple ordering which we have just described remains. To us this is the great, simple, elemental form. Here there is little to be changed. It would be impressive if the walls, which should encircle the people, actually did have the form of a ring drawn about the congregation, and if they were to merge with the roof so as to form one single dome. But this is not actually necessary, since in any case the continuing quadrilateral of the walls is "ring" and since the covering of walls and roof is itself "vault" and "shrine."

In the altar we see simply the table for the supper. Formerly Christ was seen in it—and this is certainly right but nevertheless it is difficult for us to understand. Still, if we keep to the old custom of a stone table set fast in the earth, this says very beautifully that the altar *is* the earth. And if, later on, we recognize that this earth is Christ, then the old idea proves true for us too.

The altar itself is simply a table but it is raised and emphasized by means of steps. The people stand around it in a ring and if there are more people than can be contained in one ring then they stand ring within ring, ordered concentrically. Here the people can be given articulation, for instance the adults may be put in the outermost ring, the young people in the middle ring and the children—who should indeed be closest to the Lord since they have just come from his hands—in the innermost one. In this way the people would be arranged in accordance with their sacred states and conditions. At the front, the priest would stand before the altar for the whole congregation.

We now show this design in ground-plan and cross section and we sketch in the people, for they are one of the building materials or far better, it is out of their ordering that the structure first takes form. Here we use the symbol of the open ring for the individual human being.

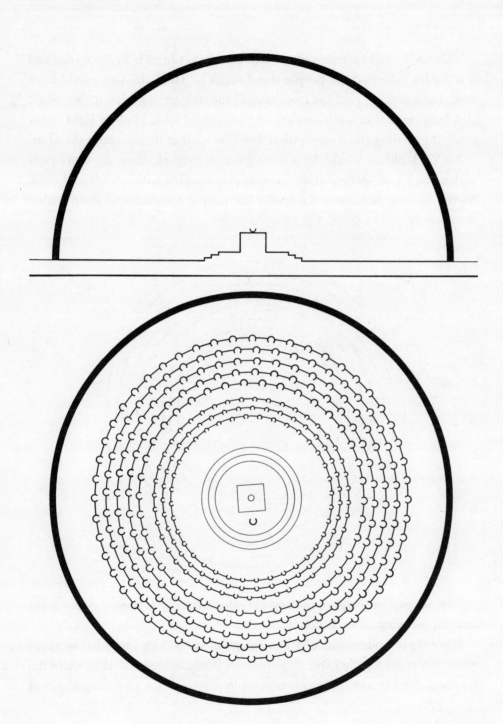

This whole structure emanates from the altar. Christ is in the center and it is for his sake that the people stand about it. The light, too, would have to emanate from it, perhaps from many candles standing upon it. We might also imagine that in addition each of the faithful would hold a light in his hand, thus letting the congregation describe a blissful ring about the altar.

Such a building would be a most genuine symbol. Here the altar rests within vault and space just as the germ lies hidden within husk and seed. Sacred secrecy permeates the space, the people are sheltered deep within the mystery.

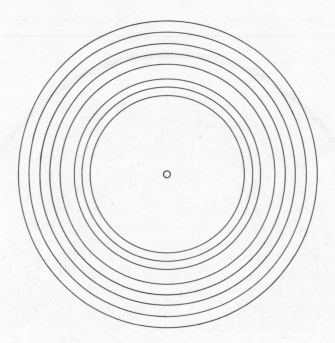

Now we shall attempt to understand what actually happens in this form and the meaning of each detail.

It is easy to understand why people gather in the ring and what happens when they come together into this common form. Indeed, all of us know the family gathering about the common table. Through the unending chain of

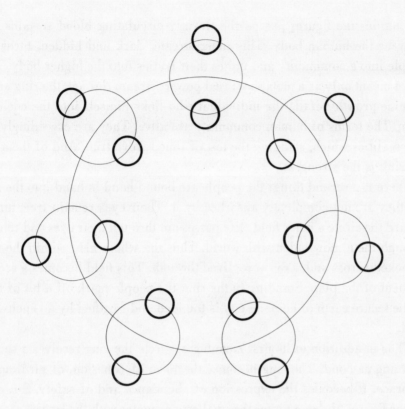

hands the ring links human being into human being. Through their hands
the individuals exchange themselves for the higher form and in doing so
they grow stronger. When people know they are at one they form the ring
in accordance with an inner law. The people gathered in the ring to hold
court, and, dancing, they form the ring in the round dance.

Ring is inviolability.

Neither beginning nor end exist in it, it begins and ends everywhere.
Bending back completely into itself, it is the strongest and the most inward
of all figures, the figure which is most at one.

Ring is also circle.

In the closed form of the ring the arc-ing movement which originated it
circles incessantly ahead, an inner stream of power which constantly renews

and unifies the figure, just as the warmly circulating blood sustains and enlivens the human body. This inner stream, dark and hidden, turns the people into a community and unites their bodies into the higher body. This is not meant only as a metaphor: real powers stream through the ring and a genuine growth befalls the individual who links himself into the common form. The forms of human community are alive. They are exceedingly potent realities which, standing the test of time, prove true. And of them all, the ring is the strongest.

There is a second thing: the people are bound hand in hand into the ring but they are not completely absorbed by it. Their eyes remain free, turned toward the circle's inner field: life passes out through their eyes and returns through them, now laden with world. Thus the whole field within the ring is looked across and, as it were, lived through. This field becomes a second element of the plan. Standing in the ring the people mark off a bit of land as the secure earth of home: a city is founded and fortified by an encircling wall.

Thus in addition to its first meaning as circle the ring receives a second meaning as bond. The ring becomes the form of cohesion, of girdling, of embrace. It becomes the expression of abundance and of safety. Since, of all the figures, the ring unites the smallest perimeter with the largest content, it is the richest and the most indwelling of them all. This is again connected with its stability, for at the perimeter the eccentric pressure of the contents is transformed into tension and it is against this tension that the ring establishes its inviolability. And so it can be said that the abundance of the inner field is transformed into the inviolability of the binding ring. Both field and perimeter are different forms of one and the same "inwardness" and both of them "mean" the same thing. Lastly, it is the same living power which is exchanged darkly through the clasped hands and openly through the eyes.

The inner field lies open to the eyes which move across it and at last, striking the ring somewhere, one pair of eyes may encounter another. In the ring everyone may look at everyone else—here in the small circle is utter

unreserve, the openness of all to all. If the lines of all these possible encounters are drawn, a network is formed, spanned between the people. This
network is the elemental form of social life and hence above all else it is
the form of spoken intercourse, of speech.

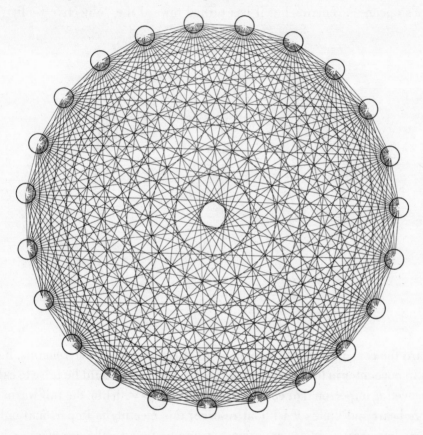

But now a third element enters: the center.

The eyes, which in themselves can look in all directions, gather together
in the altar, in the point which all eyes share. The network draws together
toward the center and changes to a star.

Now the people's togetherness takes on a stricter form. The openness of
all toward the inner space remains, of course, but now each person is com-

pletely open only for the innermost part. In it, the people are united. It is not as if each one were now to sink back again into his solitariness; the common unreserve remains and each person knows it, but he knows, too, that the true way to what lies within, into the other's heart, passes through the center. Love's openness remains but it has turned toward the "objective reality,"

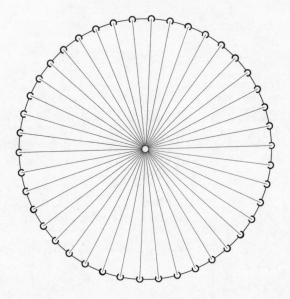

toward the center which is common to all. Even the encounter remains, but it is an encounter in the point of the shared meaning. It would be false to call this meeting impersonal or cold: each person brings with him the full warmth of his heart and yields it without reserve; this meeting is impersonal only for modern man in whose experience are to be found only strangers or intimate personal friends. Only he who does not dare to give his heart into the whole remains unmoved. This is a different form of common life from that which we know and are accustomed to but it is certainly not a lesser one. Here what we are in the habit of calling personality recedes. It is only unconsciously that the one is given to the other as a personality—his outlines are blurred, they lie beyond the focal length of the glance. This other person

is primarily the man with whom one shares what is innermost, with whom
one is, as it were, of "one heart." What he happens to look like and the things
that are unusual about him are not so very important, for the encounter
does not move from the externals into the depths—rather does it come to
pass in those depths which are shared, thence to extend out into the externals.
Probably the depths transform the externals also. Indeed, there will be little
distinctive about men who are at home in this form of common life—their
particularities will gradually disappear. The depths which they share will
pervade their faces and their bearing and they will grow similar to one another. But this will not be that similarity which results when the innermost
formative powers of men are exterminated, when the powers which illumine
them from the heart are crushed leaving only the empty shell. Rather will
it be the similarity of men who are one in the final things.

Here there are two paths from one human being to another: one path goes
through the chain of hands, the other through the center. Even neighbor and
neighbor do not see each other, but they find one another in looking to the
common center and they feel that this center makes them stretch out their
hands to each other when they look at it. If communion were based only on
the exchange from hand to hand and from eye to eye, an ordering of the
people in concentric rings would be impossible. Each ring would remain
caught up in itself and nothing could pass from one ring into the other. In
the concentric rings the eyes cannot see each other, for the man who is standing in front of me has his back to me. It is the center which really links one
ring into the other. The inner circling is transformed into the center, there
to be transformed again into the inwardness of the second ring. Or: the center spreads outward from ring to ring in a movement like that of the concentric waves caused when a stone falls into water or like the growth of trees
in rings, or like the radiation of light in expanding spheres.

The center is the ring transformed. Even that ring which is utterly caught
up in itself in inner circling produces the center as its second, its opposite
form. Its inner movement evokes the motionless pole outside and in this pole
the inner movement emerges again in another form, transposed across time

and space. The center is in the nature of the ring. This means that the strength and the warmth and the inviolability which flows through the people in the ring, linking them to each other, also make them have a common center and that in this center the selfsame communion is at one and alive once more: the center is the common heart.

It may seem astonishing that an intrinsic power, which is utterly submerged in the inwardness of its own form, can also appear in a completely different place and in a completely different form and yet remain itself— that the same power of the heart can be at once an inner circling and a motionlessness in the centermost point; that one form may turn into the other, may even require the other. It is here that the problem of form emerges. To have *living* shape means to bud forth in clear and simple form and yet to be capable of changing into a completely different one—to be sure, not into just any one, but rather into the form destined for the first—and yet through all this to remain true to oneself.

Between center and ring stretches the star-image.

The star is contained twice in the plan, once as the form of the relationship of all those who stand about to and toward the center, and again as the radiation of the center out into the ring. Through their eyes and also through the focussed attention of their whole being, the people standing about the altar create a star. This star flows from the outside inward and is dark. It is constituted by the stream of living essence which flows out through the eyes of the people. Through their eyes they yield up their very being and this surrender occurs in the form of a star-image.

Usually we understand the star only as that shining form in which a bright center spreads out into space. The dark star turns the radiant figure around, reversing it—it is into the dark star that the shining form comes home. All these human beings yield themselves into the center point and at the same time they yield up their land, the district across which they look: all this passes into the center and the center becomes the abundance and the essence of all these things. The whole globe is gathered in the tiny point. Then the light from the altar, with all that it implies, gives answer to the surrender

of the dark star-image. In the answer the shining star streams forth and gives itself in all its fullness to the space.

We know the star-image as the world's light-form. Every visible thing is clothed with stars. The focal point in the eye is also star: here the seen world is gathered into the space of a point whence it irradiates the horizon of the retina. But all this is only a reflection of the sun. Only in the sun is the earthly star made whole—in the sun which hovers free in space, shedding her light in all directions. The sun completes the earthly star in two ways: she closes its openness and she forms it, together with all the other open stars, into a radiance round about herself.

Nuptially the plant changes into blossom, and here, too, we see what "star" means. Plants are built in accordance with the spiral line—their growing is composed of the vertical movement of trunk or stem, the radial movement of the branches and of a slow circling. Thus the star-image makes a hidden contribution to plant form. When we look directly into the crown of a plant, tracing the vertical growth with our eye, we discover in it the star-image. Blossoming, the whole plant becomes a star. The vertical movement comes to a standstill, all life becomes radiance. At the same time the greenness turns to glowing color. It has been said that all this serves the process of fertilization and is intended to attract. This is correct but it is purely descriptive and is not an explanation. Nor is there much to explain. Seen from within, this plant is now a star, and to be a star means to be still, to be luminous and radiant, to have a center and to stream forth out of it; to be a star means to illumine the world, to bless it and to bewitch it—it means to be shot through and through with radiance.

From this, we may derive the meaning of the dark, inverted star; its meaning is the opposite from that of the light star—a returning home, dusk, a gathering in of self, the surrender of spatiality, and at bottom it means dying.

The wish to explain such forms is forbidden us. They are the great fundamental ideas of creation and cannot be traced further back. They have their being prior to all explanation. Their existence has consequences which we may discover and it asserts something to which we may harken. If we collect these assertions, our understanding reaches deep into the meaning of the form, but we do not in this way arrive at an explanation. The things may be compared and classified according to their forms, since wherever the same form appears, the same condition exists, and to discover this is blissful insight. This order can be praised in poetry, for indeed it is the task of poetry to gather the things together in forms of unity. They can be joined architecturally, for the art of building rests on the fact that in their changing structural forms the things of the world may be compared to one another and to the mathematical figures. The forms can even be turned to good account technically. We can rely on them in every way since they are not allegories whose meaning has been agreed upon: they are the powerful figures which build the world. Finally, they can be ordered in systems, for they possess their logical inner sequence in accordance with which one figure grows out of the other. Each form is so constructed that, although it is utter "condition," complete in itself, yet at the same time it presupposes that a particular form went before it and that a second particular form will follow after it. The whole sequence of such inwardly connected phases is itself again form, form unfolded into time. This was first discovered in the beautiful sequence found in plant growth, which begins with the sphere of the seed gathered up into itself in an inwardness devoid of time and which then bursts forth, shooting up into stalks, finally to spread out in a tracery of leaves and branches. At last the growth ceases, time stands still and out of the plant the star shines. Afterward the growth retreats to the inside and swelling inwardly ripens the fruit. Its very essence declares: this plant has become a star. There can be no higher assertion than this.

It would be meaningless to ask why the star is found in our plan. Since we find it there we do well to assume that the star is one of the elemental forms under which men meet the Lord. The star is one of the sacred forms—that is all. And the meaning of this sacred form is told by its natural images, by the visible things, by the eye, the flowers, the stars. It would be equally meaningless to ask why the ring or the center are found in this form; but we may understand ever more profoundly what ring and center mean.

Ring, center and star are interrelated, the one grows out of the other. The circling movement produces the motionless pole, the pole the circling movement. The dark star condenses into the center which in turn unfolds as a light star. This may be compared to breathing: it is as if earth and people were being breathed in and out from the center.

The completed figure is the structural image of the inhabited earth: it renders people and land in the form of the spoked wheel.

Our plan contains as its fifth and sixth element the sphere. The sphere arches over the spoked wheel as shell and fills this shell as swelling space.

The sphere is to the solid bodies what the ring is to the plane figure. Full abundance within, everywhere convex without, it is the most inward of all bodies, combining the greatest content with the smallest extent. Therefore it is the form of all security in space. From the little amoeba, balling itself

into a tiny sphere to the sun within the universe all things which want to be
alone, all things which withdraw, all things which seek safety, assume the
form of the sphere. The sphere is the form of inwardly sheltered riches and
of the gathered whole. Of all the figures, it is the most invulnerable, for it
erects the greatest resistance against attacks from the outside and holds its
content most securely together. Lastly, like the ring, the sphere is an unfolding
from the center and a return to it. The sphere is the form of expanding light.
In the succession of forms through time, the sphere stands at the beginning.
The creatures themselves develop out of it and at the end are gathered up
into it once more. It is the form of seed and fruit, of beginning and of consummation. In this connection the sphere is comparable to the "one" among
numbers: it is the form of all those things which are designated with "one,"
of all oneness, of all inwardness. It could almost be said, and indeed it has
often been said, that the architectural dome is the form of a people's inwardness and that beneath this form a people is complete unto itself like a heavenly body in space. The dome is thought to be the image of national unity.

   This is false. A human community cannot turn itself into a sphere, like a
drop of water or a star. Human society is ordered horizontally. The sphere
is forbidden it. And here the community is differentiated from the individual
and from mankind. The sphere is given to the individual, his body forms it
as eye, as cupped hand, as head. Indeed, his skeleton reveals a double
structure: delicate, movable, far-stretched limbs carry the head which
crowns the body, round like a star and arched to a glorious dome. The head
is like the sun. In mankind, living all around the globe, the sphere closes
once more. Those mythologies which consider men to be the delicate outermost organs of the living earth may or may not be right, but in any case
mankind as a whole is ordered spherically by the surface of the earth. And
this fact of being bent back on ourselves must surely form our feeling about
our existence in some way. Ever since our systems of communication have
shortened distances and laid their net about the earth, we moderns have
begun to realize that mankind inhabits a globe. Perhaps such experiences
are the beginning of a geographical architecture of the future whose concern

will be the whole of mankind. In any case, the community and the nation, since they are neither the individual nor the whole, cannot assume the spherical form. The form of the community's solidarity is the circle on the earth's surface. (And beyond this there is the assuredly strong form of the human gathering which is hollowed into the vale or raised up into the mountain.) The peoples live in circles next to each other.

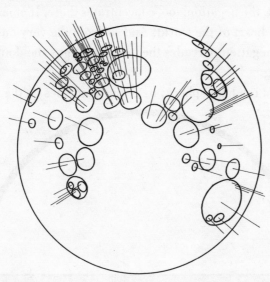

Thus the dome—and every habitable space contains the vault—does not mean the nation. Far more does it signify the universe and her firmament: that great space up into which life radiates and which in turn affects the earth, that space up into which men grow, which they see through and yet do not inhabit, which is accessible to life and yet not its dwelling—the place of the clouds, the winds and the stars, and the great vault which surrounds them.

Our whole building thus represents the whole world and repeats the wisdom of her structure. The floor is the surface of the earth, the home of men; the space vaulting above it is that great space which lies next to life; and the firmament terminates both. This limit holds the earth, is the shrine of the world. It is simple end, the impenetrable. Its consummately concave form evades every grip, is incomprehensible. No light penetrates it. To be sure, we sense its course in the dull reflection of the light which diffuses out from the center until striking it, but what we actually see is the light's inner extension—the empty form itself is ever dark, the absolute end, the "no." And this negation is effective for out from the boundary it pervades everything sheltered within the vault and since the whole world is united in the centermost point, the negation, too, concentrates there. It emerges once more in the innermost heart of the world. And so from the very outside and from the very inside negation pervades the universe. Thus the dome is at last the great foreboding.

The firmament is a hemisphere; its center point lies on the earth's surface

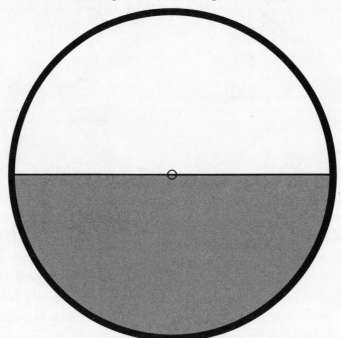

where we stand. Beneath us the figure grows unclear. We cannot actually say that the hemisphere continues on as level land from where we are standing, thus closing the universe, for what lies beneath the earth, the depths and the force of gravity, are not completely inaccessible to us either. Gravity pervades the structure and in addition the foundations of the building reach down into the earth. Therefore we may well compare the depths of the earth to the universe. Then the figure receives a second half which is dark and heavy, and the firmament continues at the very bottom of the earth, far, far below in the abyss.

It could be said that this design and its interpretation are archaic: for a long time our earth has not been a disk, floating on a dark sea, domed by the firmament. Rather is she a tiny star journeying through the silent universe. This may be correct astronomically. The plan is archaic, since it shows world "in beginning." (Or is it really wrong? Does not a new firmament stand out in sharp relief for us today in the far, far distance, its endless radius delimiting our universe? And is not the earth even today a sphere? Why do we deduce from our astronomical insight only that the world is lost and forlornly alone in the universe, forgetting that she is gloriously rounded? How beautifully conceived are the old representations in which the ripe apple of the earth rests in the hand of God the Father, or the symbol of the imperial apple with its little cross in the hand of the Christian emperor!) But what has the building art to do with astronomy? To build obviously does not mean to encamp at some theoretical standpoint, thence to make people happy with mathematical constructions. Rather does it mean to clarify and to form a human situation. Architecture is not concerned with how the world might be imagined "in the abstract" but only with how, here and now, it is real to these particular people. There are old examples which are apparently based on some speculations as to the absolute meaning of the sphere and they show what happens when one tries to build the theoretical form of an abstract world. Among them is the Roman Pantheon. This great circular structure is designed around a sphere which barely touches the earth. Its upper half is a dome and in place of the lower half stands a cylinder.

This structure may have been intended for the gods or for the sacred All but it is in any case unfit for men. If we seek out its structural scheme, we discover a ball rolling on a level plain. The comparisons which might occur to us are quite banal: we are reminded of the game where two teams amuse

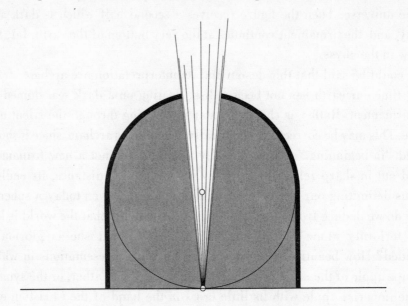

themselves with a tremendous ball, or of a captive balloon held fast on ropes. In any event the space hangs in mid-air. In order to understand it we would have to climb up a ladder into its center. Nevertheless the structure is impressive and this is simply because it is not fully carried out. The source of light is not in the center point but in the crown of the dome and hence the structure is not a sphere at all: a second pattern is intermixed with the spherical one. This second idea had succeeded more clearly and beautifully in Mycaenae long before: there the dome itself stands directly on the earth and light falls into it from above. This scheme is genuine world-image for in it world—and world, not as the brain constructs it but as men people it— is erected into majestic form.

There is something else which architecture obviously cannot achieve, and herein lies its modern danger: it cannot satisfy the expectations of an aestheticism which is entirely caught up in its own subjective isolation. The works of architecture are communal forms and the individual cannot understand them as long as he is alone. These works are produced by the community and, indeed, it is in bringing them forth that the community proves itself to be a unity. Only out of the community can they be understood. To build does not mean to solve mathematical problems nor to create pleasing spaces: it means to place great communal forms before God. As remote from the subjective as from the abstract, in the strict and exalted canon of the great forms, true architecture dwells.

The structure given in this first plan represents world, world "in beginning," world which is still at rest in its very center. Within this center everything is present once more in transformed form. The universe is at one in the innermost spot. This, then, is center: the common heart, the going out and the coming home of all things, that infinite within out of which life is lived and to which it returns. Here is the "hidden shrine" of the universe. And hence it is that to enter into the center means to go into the whole, into the undivided, into the unbroken.

Some men have gone this way. They went into the inside and finally they came almost to the innermost point. There they found everything together: all the creatures, the human beings, the nations, mankind, all habitable land, the depths of the earth and the heights of the heavens, the stones and the stars. They saw all things in unbroken unity, and then they lost sight of the distinctions. Everything became one and the same to them, this was that and everything was nothing. Afterward, when they returned, they no longer understood the real world. To them, she seemed deceptive—it could only be a delusion that she contained the things in varied forms. And so their counsel was to leave the forms and to enter into the center, for it is there that the world abides. This was assuredly a confusion. It is loving union which takes place in the innermost heart and which confirms our entering into it. The union of love occurs when differing beings yield themselves to a common form. But union is not identification—it is embrace and mutual exchange; the things which so lovingly unite remain particular creatures, and afterward, when the time of inwardness and intimacy is over, each goes enriched to his own particular place.

Others went still farther. They too entered the "hidden shrine" and took part in the great union. But they pressed forward into the very innermost area and there they found the great foreboding. In the very center they encountered the great negation: the kernel of this world was empty and it harbored the void.

The ways of worldly mysticism are forlorn paths. They lead into an ever denser world and end at the rim of the void. Ultimately they afford us the view onto the horizon of emptiness.

All secular building about a center is work without hope. The ring and the dome are the most desolate of all forms. They remain forever a circling trapped in itself, forever mere casting, a casting which rises up at the beginning, reaches its apex and finally falls back into gravity, just as natural life bends back to the earth. Their space is forever the cave. The true meaning of the arch, its whole impetus and its weighty earthiness, must be learned from the most pagan of all buildings, from those of the Romans.

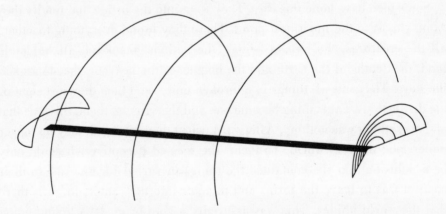

When Christianity came into the world, the arch lost its power. The Christians no longer recognized themselves in it, and for them the arch became opening and passage. In varied repetition the Christian arch encircles the decisive spot where the sacred way pierces a wall, the spot where, as portal, it opens up a new space. Like the electric current which polarizes the rod it encircles, the girdling arch accompanies and strengthens the progress of the way.

Christianity shattered the centric type of building and at the same time established it anew. But this new centric building no longer serves the mystical intensification of the world's inwardness: it is itself sacred process.

This occurs in the following way:

At first the congregation gathers in the ring. In reality, however, it is the Lord who unites the people so. Then, through their eyes and speech the people surrender themselves into the center. Under the image of the dark star they renounce the world and make it flow back to its origin. But what then takes place upon the altar is not poetic mysticism: it is Christian sacrifice. The former reaches the innermost point of this world, only to be the more her captive; the latter quits this world to enter the eternal.

In the sacrifice the world sinks inward into a still more inner innermost, but she does not sink forever. In the very center, endlessly far within, lies the inner limit like the rim of an open well. And there, where the earth ends, God's heaven begins. The world's hidden shrine lies empty for heaven and, praying, the people set foot on the eternal threshhold. Now they understand what it means that the Lord is "in their midst." He is with them. His prayer is directed to the Father in his inward heaven and the people are taken up into the movement of this prayer as if into an endless vortex. There they discover the way out. This holy way quits the earth to go toward God. The people sink into the eternal abyss and there they share in the birth of the Son into time. As a tiny secret spark, the new light of the world is kindled.

Now all forms fall into their sacred-natural order: the new light shines into the hearts of men, a blessed ring encircles the altar, sacred world is born and each individual becomes a star. The world has become God's innocent child, confirming the Lord's promise that all who believe on his name may become children of God.

All this the Lord meant when he said that he wished to be in the midst of those who gather together in his name. His name—this is the word by

which the Father calls him. He could also have said: "in my power," or simply, "in me." When he pledges his desire to be in the midst of men, to be their center, he is saying that he wants to gather them together even at the very beginning, that he wants to bind their ring, to mark out for them a sacred home, and that he wants to be that light which illumines every man who is in this world. He wishes to bless the land and to found a new world over it. And, as the new sun, he wishes to fill this world with light to its uttermost limits.

In part we can understand what occurs when the few gather in his name,
The light shines in the darkness and the darkness comprehends it; the Lord
comes unto his own and his own receive him. A holy city is founded and
the sacred universe is created anew. In these few the land and all space
beneath the heavens become one single, sacred body. The earth is united
with the Lord. She drinks his holy cup and eats him as bread.

The spoked wheel, or, as was formerly said, the rose, becomes the image

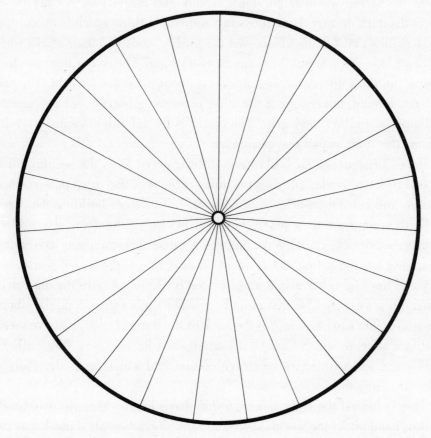

of the Lord and of his body. (This is more than a comparison, for the earth
is truly in flower, truly aflame.) This figure says that the Lord has become
the boundary, the center, the abundance of all things; that all things spring

from him, all things flow to him, all things abide in him. All things are in him and he in them; the structure is one great body of the Lord and the rose the image of his sacred stronghold. The world is in creation.

But what of the vault? Is not the vault the end of this new world, too? What lies within it is opened to the inside, looking to the center. But at the back, the dark boundary runs its course and it closes in a ring. The vault spans the sacred world impervious, remote and indivisible. No ray penetrates the dark destiny. Is not the vault something third which is masked in mystery like that fate to which even the ancient gods and their works were subject? Does it not annul the center in everything? The center lies infinitely inside, the vault utterly outside, darkness about the radiant world. The one is light, a point, utterly open; the other is receding horizon, a consummate hollowness eluding every grip. The center is the infinite inwardness of the things, the vault withdrawn perimeter.

Here Christian centric building is differentiated from the secular for a second time. In secular building the dome is the end, that third power which bounds and rules the world from without. In Christian building the dome is God's second dwelling place. For God is also as the dome shows him: utterly withdrawn, impalpable, infinitely remote, consummate concavity, the rising and the setting, the dawn and the evening of the sacred world, her day and her night, her origin and her death. He is not only the answer to heart-felt prayer but also that mute Fate which arches providentially above the world, that Christian fate at the back of the things and high above them, that fate beneath which Christ also stood when he spoke of "the Father's will"—the will with which he struggled and into which he finally yielded himself: "into the Father's hands."

That is indeed the right image, the Father's hands. This vault is God's hollow hand about the world, sheltering and pervading all things; it is the retina of his dark and open eye which, watching over the world in ceaseless creation, recognizes her and provides for her. In this image God is at once deep within the innermost ring and far outside in the periphery. In between

lie universe, earth and men, placed between God and God. But probably
both periphery and center are the same thing. Out of God's solitude the
innermost heart returns: the antitheses are at one.

We sense the final, purely theological meaning of this plan. Dark and
remote God's providence arches, and in the innermost center it gives birth
to the radiant child. Where the child's light streams out into the darkness,
sacred earth is born. What lies between—people, land and universe—is
embedded in the Father's movement to the child and in the reflux of thanks.
So perhaps the profoundest meaning of this plan is that it takes the people
up into the sacred river of eternity, into the river which bears them from
the Father to the Son and back once more, a new race.

When the holy centric form stands, as it were, quietly before us, closed
in on all sides and so beautifully ordered, some may be tempted to believe
that it is based in itself and that, in the worldly sense, we may rely upon it.
But this is a serious error. It is dangerous to praise the strength and the
reliability even of the sacred world, for if we do this God's eye may close
over it and it may pass away; or it may turn from God and degenerate into
the hard and empty form of the pagan world. The closed form is lasting as
long as it remains open—this is the paradox of Christian centric building.
It is lasting as long as God creates it from within and watches over it lovingly
from without. In God alone is it eternal. Only that form which is borne by
the Eternal One is "eternal form." All else is error.

Here I would like to introduce a design which I made many years ago
but which I have not previously published. It shows how variously we may
interpret the essential form of Christian centric building.

Here an oval was chosen for the ground plan: the form was drawn out
toward the back and as a result the center moved forward. In this center we
placed the altar. Out of it rose a high column which spread out as it ascended, then changed into an arch, and finally fell away over the congregation down to the periphery. It would be possible to emphasize this movement through the lighting. The lighting should be indirect and should illu-

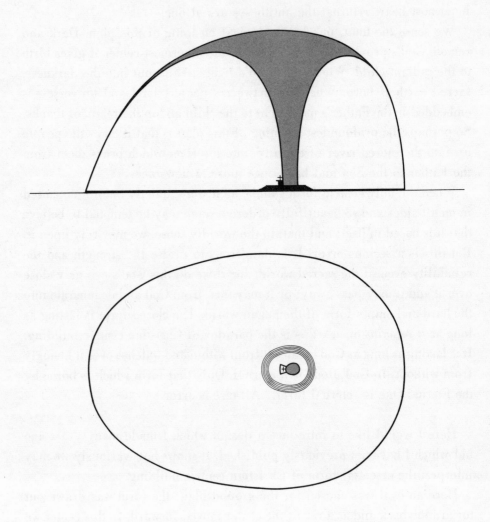

mine altar and pillar in the most brilliant light, then lose in intensity as it reaches farther up and finally fade with the falling away of the vaulting. We thought of varying this type of lighting; for instance the brightest zone could be transferred either into the dome or to the outer perimeter. With the help of the light, the space could in a sense be created ever anew out of nothing and could be made to ebb and flow together with the act of worship. Thus the building should originate out of the center. It should imitate the movement of a fountain, ascending bright and luminous then to unfold over the congregation and finally to fall down at their back. The consummate palpability and object-ivity of the pillar should continually merge with the consummate concavity of the vaulting.

The real difficulty in this design lies in the fact that there is no room for the center. It is at the very center that the inwardly intensifying movement of the space strikes the solid shaft of the column. This difficulty is perceptible as soon as we try to find a place for the altar. Actually the atlar should be built into the column, for indeed it is the column's movement which produces it. But since this is not possible, the altar must somehow be put in front of the pillar or built around it. The pillar is a solid object—it is like the trunk of a tree beneath whose crown the people gather. We might be reminded of the ancient world-tree. But here it is not the people who make up this tree— they do not carry out the movement themselves. They are relieved of it and instead it is carried out by the building as their representative. The whole arrangement is very "objective": the people stand looking on before an architectural happening.

Such designs show the richness of the centric form. Here we have tried to represent the welling forth of the firmament out of the world's innermost point. For this purpose we made use of the fountain-form whose movement upturns the pillar to form the vaulting. As early as the Middle Ages this form had produced incomparably beautiful spaces such as that of the Marienburg refectory. Although this form provides a good sculptural like-ness of the relationship between center and perimeter, it contains one diffi-culty which we must accept: for the simple reason that it is a likeness, this form prevents the people from carrying out the movement themselves. One

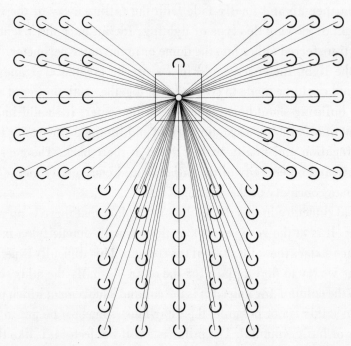

element of our plan was chosen as the starting point for a particular design.

Conversely, the plan may also be abbreviated. Certain elements are then left out. Not long ago one of these abbreviated forms provoked a great deal of discussion—the one in which the people stand only on three sides of the altar and the priest on the fourth, but in which all turn to face the altar as the common center. In very small congregations the abbreviation may go even farther, with the people standing on only one side of the altar and the priest on the other. Here indeed we reach that limit where, out of the ring a two-fold division, a "standing-opposite," develops, so that the mutilated form is no longer able to represent its true meaning.

In this way it was sought to revive an old usage; the name "christocentric" was invented for this and although it is certainly not very satisfactory it at least clearly says that Christ should stand in the center.

When we draw in the lines of vision we immediately recognize the inner condition of this ordering. Even though some of its rays are lacking and the

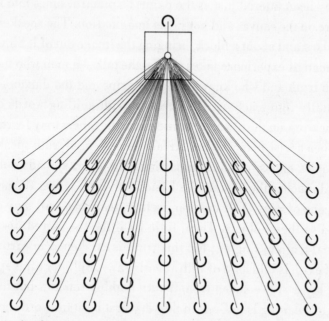

empty places in the ring must somehow be bridged, the star is still present.

The peculiar danger of such abbreviations is that they can easily shift into the forms of discourse. In the first place every divine service actually does contain elements of a dialogue between priest and people; and in addition these two basic forms are externally so similar that a group may instantly assume the second form when the service itself shifts into address or dialogue. The people need not change their positions for this to happen but the inner meaning of the form changes.

"Discourse" means the gradual working out of a truth which is revealed step by step, in address, answer and reply. The discourse is begun in the direction of the intuitively anticipated truth. A first reserved word is spoken toward it, this calls forth a second, and gradually, word by word, out of the very first word the last is brought forth, the new. Apart from the speech of ultimate revealing in which the speakers speak out their innermost being themselves, and which is akin to the final looking of eye into eye, the speech of discourse is not directed at the speakers. Rather is it directed at the truth which lies in between them. The new truth emerges out of the words which have already been uttered just as the painter's picture comes into being as a new creature on the canvas and not in his imagination. The speakers are like sculptors who stand about a block, bringing the image out of it blow by blow.

When a man of experience takes part in the talk—a man who has already found much truth and who knows the good grips and the dangers—the talk turns gradually into teaching. He directs it with guiding words or he may take over the work on the block by himself and the others may learn in watching him. When a wise man who has already experienced truth speaks, the discourse becomes exposition and imparting. The word spreads out from the speaker and reaches the hearers. Its basic form is no longer the network but rather the cone of rays. A discussion, lecture, teaching—all may commence toward God as their subject. Then, little by little, the sacred discourse sets God's eternal truth to ringing; but this truth is awakened in earthly matter. The stuff of earth is laid hold of with attentive awe. Splinter after splinter and layer after layer are removed from it until nothing remains but the creature whose single meaning is in God. In the very first hesitant word the discourse contains the truth just as the block "contains" the statue—but for this very reason it is never prayer. The man who prays possesses nothing. He gives everything he has away and waits on the Lord; he does not keep the earth as material nor even as creature—he does not even keep his own createdness. He yields himself without reserve into the hands of God. Discourse consummates the world, prayer offers it in sacrifice.

There are parts of the divine service in which priest and people speak with one another. These are short words of encouragement or instruction and they are like the calls between workmen engaged in a common task. The divine service also contains teaching and this lies close to the form of discourse. The remaining words are either words of prayer or words of ministry. These words go "through Christ" toward God as their single partner, or they come from God through Christ to the people. Thus the divine service contains two layers of speech. One of them is the speech of discourse, but the structure of the great words of prayer toward God completely overshadows it. Little takes place between priest and people, almost everything between these two and God. The priest who stands facing the people at the altar speaks the words of prayer into it as if into a center which opens into the infinite. When he ministers the word he should do so from out of the center, for instance by going to the inner side of the altar table and down a step, turning there to face the people. Only the short vocations and responses may be exchanged *across* the altar. For this produces the dialogue-form and then there is danger that the divine service may turn into discourse and forfeit its star-form.

Our plan will not always remain as it is now—it contains germs of later growth. These are still sunk deep into the centric pattern but they will grow tall and will burst it asunder.

Let us imagine a divine service in this space. The people have closed in the ring and the priest goes to the altar. He enters the room at a particular point and thence he makes his way to the center. Of all the innumerable ways which might lead inside from the perimeter he selects this particular one and by his choice he honors it above all the others. Then he remains standing on one side of the altar. He can only stand on one side, but by standing on this particular side and on no other, he shows it favor. He lifts his voice and his eyes, looking across the altar and beyond it, and thus he continues that way on which he has already embarked. In doing all this, in merely entering the room, in going forward to the center, in simply stand-ing, then in raising his eyes and beginning to speak or to move his hands in one of the acts of worship—in all this he would constantly mark out a par-ticular direction and continue a way, and by means of this way he would intersect the round form. For he could do all this only as that which he is, a human creature who has a life story, an origin and a destination and who is sent on the way from the one to the other, knowing that this way leads from God to God and that therefore it is "sacred way." It is given to the human body to go this way. This is indeed the body's spiritual meaning and the meaning of its facing into the remote distance.

The individual who is placed in the center pierces the ring a second time vertically. His stance prepares the way for a movement which quits the sacred land and the circle of its horizon to go straight up. He introduces an ascending motion, or, more accurately, he indicates the direction in which the space might at some time burst asunder if the center, which is now at rest within itself, were to become the hub of an axis about which the spoked wheel circled.

Through his simple stance this one man expresses what all dimly sense. Each feels the pull of the earth and the overpowering ascent of life, each senses that he has been sent on a journey and also that another pair of eyes would meet his own, were he to lift them from the center. All this will one day come to pass but the time is not yet ripe for it. All ways still lead inward, all eyes still meet at the heart and the man who stands closest to the center bends low over it, sheltering it as it were in himself. He speaks into it with lowered voice and when he speaks to those standing about him, his words are gathered deep and come from the innermost center. He is embedded in the centric form and does not know of his own stance nor does he know that he himself is an individual. It is still deep in the night. The Lord is a child lying in the manger and the little congregation rejoices at his birth. Mary is seated there with her young child on her lap. With arms and eyes she embraces him. In her bliss that she may so embrace the Lord, does she perhaps forget that this child will soon learn to walk and that he must go a difficult road to a terrible end? Lost in gazing at the child so rapt in bliss, perhaps she perceives the light which shines out from his very heart and perhaps she forgets everything else at the sight of it. (But she does not forget. Mary is sorrowful in bliss and her eyes gaze out into the far distance.)

Everything is still asleep in the germ and the things are still lying close together, illumined by an inward light. Nothing has as yet cut through this first plan to disturb it but already there are contained in it the powers which will one day rend it asunder—the commandment to grow and to burst the dome. The time of bliss is short and when it is over man stands again in the sun, amidst the things, conscious of his body and of its meaning. He realizes that he is alone and that he has been sent on a far journey.

Sacred Parting

The Open Ring

W<small>E SEEK</small> the basic form of every day, the space of awakened men who stand in the midst of time and who have been sent out into history, who know that although they have a home, they still must travel a road, who know that they have themselves and the sacred congregation and Christ in its center, but who know, too, that Christ is speaking with the Father "in heaven." We seek the form of the church between the times, the form of the sprouting seed, of the coming kingdom.

The childhood of the Lord does not last long. It stands at the very beginning and it is soon over. The last supper is the average situation of every day. Christ sits with his own at table, he is seated in their midst and he gives them food. He is with them, but he is also with the Father and with that which is to come. With the Father in heaven. He introduces his own to him and, pleading that not one of them may be lost, he blesses them in the Father's name. The ring of people at the table is in a sense closed and the Lord is truly within it; but at the same time, out from the heart of the Lord, it is opened wide to the Father.

Leonardo fills the table on one side and at both ends—in front of Christ himself the table is empty. This is the proper image of this evening. As long as men have still to go their way, any everyday fellowship allowed to them will be that of the open ring: the ring is almost closed but not entirely—one segment remains open. Christ is in the middle, he reaches out his hands to right and left and the disciple may rest on his bosom. But he himself looks to the open side into the remoteness of the Father before whom he enters in, holding the people on each hand. Their prayers unite with his and they ask that the Father may grant fulfillment "through Christ." Thus Christ is in the same room with his own and yet he is not—he belongs at the same time to another space, he is at once middle and mediator.

The plan which we now present is intended to be valid for the average situation of every day and year. It is more difficult than the first plan since elements which were formerly hidden in the germ now emerge, enriching and encumbering the design. This plan is meant to weave into a unity inwardness and remoteness, a sheltering and an opening up, existence and way, and it is meant to open up a space into the infinite. But for this very reason it is more true to the average situation for the average situation is indeed difficult.

In this plan, too, the people stand in a ring about the altar, again the sheltering dome arches over both of them and again the priest stands at the altar as the representative of the congregation. He looks out to the east, into the openness, for it is there that the space opens: the people step back freeing one sector, the vault gapes in a tremendous window. Resplendent emptiness reaches in to the altar. Thus this altar, too, belongs to the congregation for it stands in their very center; but it is exactly at this point that the interrupting gap begins, at the heart of the people's space. Thus the altar is both apex and threshhold, the center and the place of transition. This gap is itself radiant with light since the whole room has only this one window; but the gap is impenetrable for this window is vista, not gateway—that part of the world which we may tread ends at the altar.

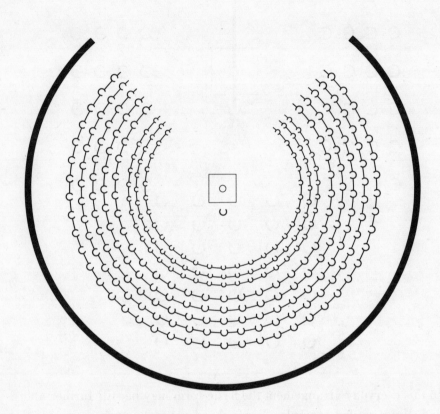

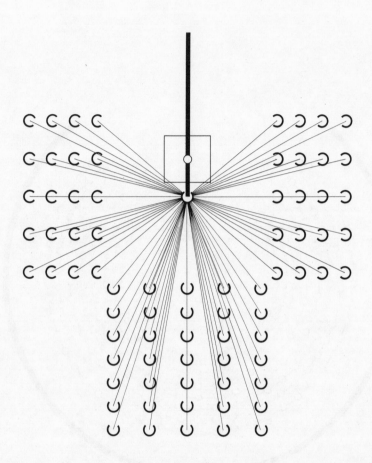

In this everyday arrangement the basic form may be still further abbreviated. We may, for example, divide the people into three groups so that
the T-form is produced. As long as the priest stands on this side of the altar
and as long as the space beyond it remains empty, the basic form is preserved, even when only a very small group stands on a single side.

To be sure, this final form of simplification gradually begins to change
into that other form in which the people are "on their way."

The meaning of this plan is parting, setting forth.

This plan raises to lasting condition the moment in which the closed form

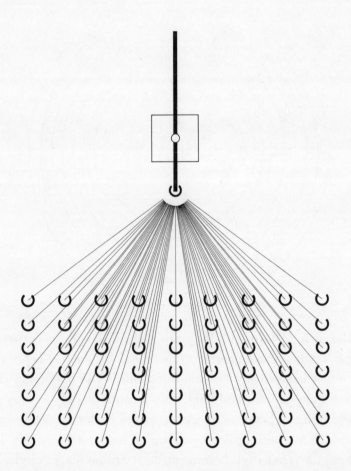

"parts," bursts open. The people are on the point of going out into the openness, they wish to take the first step but they tarry a moment "on the threshhold" between security and the way. The sheltering forms are still at hand but
now they have broken open and are beginning to disappear—they are no
longer valid. The way is already at hand but at this moment the people have
not yet entered upon it and hence it is still impassable.

Breached are the original forms.

The people still stand in the ring, looking to the center, but as they look
they know that their union is in dissolution. At one place it is already severed. That which still binds the people to one another is like the last pressure

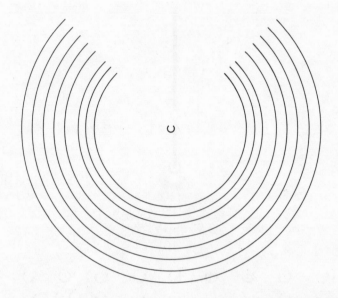

of the hand in fond farewell. They are still filled with tenderness toward one another yet this is no longer permitted them, for the way is pressing. The ultimate union has already become impossible. The dissolving ring-form can no longer close, circle and bind. This it could do only as long as it was at once beginning and end, as long as it curved back completely into itself. The ring which has been broken open can no longer achieve this. It can no longer close, for it has itself become open, it can no longer circle, for it no longer flows back into itself, it can no longer bind, for its bond is rent. With two arms it reaches out into the emptiness and at both ends a new form emerges: the point.

"Point" means to overflow, to press forward, to shine in radiance: this happens when plants force forth new shoots, this happens in sword and spear, in pinnacle and spire—through a point a tension is discharged. Out of both ends the ring's inner power overflows into the open place. The whole meaning of its form is consumed in an attempt to close up the opening but even so this is not achieved. The form remains open. And so the open ring is the form of inwardness bleeding to death. Deep in his heart each man

feels the change. Each individual is himself opened, and he understands
the meaning of the words: "heart-rending farewell."

The star is changed. A remnant of it still remains: the people look to

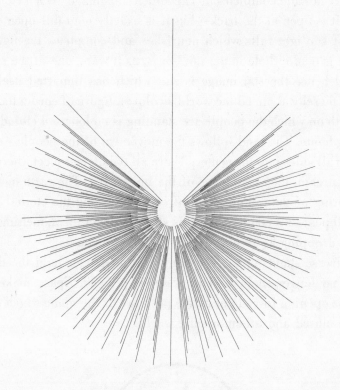

the altar and form the dark star. But in the center they see their advocate
who is looking out into the open. He gathers the centric movement and bears
it forward. Taking it up, he guides it into the open place. This whole figure
no longer sinks like the genuine star into the heart of its inwardness. Instead
it flows out of the center toward the outside.

The light, too, is still streaming out from the altar to the people but the
altar is no longer its real source: the altar itself is now only the place where
the light breaks in, the place where it is turned, handed on, imparted.

This is no longer the genuine star-image which, from within, casts its light in all directions. Here we find rather the "open star," that figure which presents itself when sunlight falls on a visible object: its surface is transformed into a mass of stars and each of these is in turn "dependent" on the sun which nourishes and completes it. The "open star-image" is not complete on all sides. It is open at the back—but it is exactly onto this open side that that ray of sunlight falls which nourishes and completes the figure. The star-image is made whole in the sun—it is, as it were, one of the sun's outposts. And hence the star-image is sun which has imparted itself to the world and thereby assumed the world's color: a figure of encounter.

The earth on which the people are standing is no longer a closed and all-embracing home. The land follows the movement of the people's eyes and flows from all sides into the center. There all tributaries meet, there, united to a great stream, they take leave of the inner area. The earth has become the wellspring of the infinite, hem of coastline along the eternal sea. The people still possess a country, but it is slipping from them, melting beneath their feet, dropping away on all sides into the openness.

The universe stands open. The dome can no longer hold the things together, it no longer shelters. The vessel is pierced. Space makes it exit through the opening forced out by the pressure of the dome which once had sealed the closed and all-embracing world.

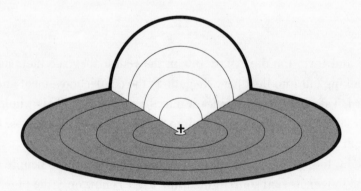

Breached is even the innermost center.

Let us not be deceived. The previous plan did not show that which is sometimes called "immanence" and this one does not show what is called "transcendence." In the very middle of the first plan lay the world's innermost place, a tiny ring, and the earth flowed to it from all sides. Inside, this ring was empty, the world was the rim of eternity's wellspring and at the very heart God dwelt alone. The waters of the earth rushed into this inner abyss, the ring enchased the sacred source of the world; creation spread out in circling waves and round about the land grew green. If we think of this center as the innermost space of the world, it is like a little tabernacle. The innermost shrine of the world stands empty for the Lord.

In the second plan this shrine has, as it were, been turned on its side. It now stands at right angles to the surface of the earth and its horizon, and it cuts this surface along a sharp edge. This is the "threshhold" between earth and heaven. Thus the inner ring where the earth once bordered the eternal has now become the hem of coastline, the edge of the waterfall. The inner boundary stretches out across the land along this threshhold: it unfolds in great portals as the boundary of the universe. And of these portals at least one becomes visible as that final line where the firmament was cut off: the casement of eternity and within it "emptiness." But basically this plan differs little from the first. The dwelling place of heaven, sheltered at the beginning deep in the innermost heart, has now come forth: the hidden openness of the world's center has become visible.

In this new plan all the things which belong to a perfect world are still at hand, but although everything still stands in its rightful place, although everything still possesses its old form, yet everything has been annulled, everything has become impossible. The form has an open place where the rings stand open, where the universe is severed, where the vault is pierced; and yet nothing more happens here than that the cohesive whole which was once so beautiful is now rent asunder. The world is opened up and negated. But she is not constituted anew. There could be a new meaning if, for example, the dark vault were to melt back from the opening and everything were to be warm in the light. But this does not happen. The old form is preserved and yet it can no longer exist. Negated, rent asunder, continually made impossible, it must yet endure. The figures still retain their original form and, indeed, this can only be understood as the commandment to uphold their original meaning. But the world can no longer live up to this commandment. And so she seeks her original cohesion: her entire inner meaning is transformed into the urge for restoration, into a striving for completion which seeks to bridge the gap. Living power streams from the sundered whole, the entire form begins to move out into the open, there to meet with emptiness. The form is bleeding.

The form of this world is wounded. Its bonds stand open, its meaning is impossible. Everything that it wants to do, everything that it should do is prevented it. From the very boundary to the innermost heart yawns a great wound and even the center itself is a shattered vessel. All forms of this time are open. They are like thin vessels struck by a blow from without which has pierced their walls and churned their contents into a storm-tossed sea; the outline of the forms is the final wave of surf upon the shore. Or they are like caves into which a ray of sunlight falls.

Now the form of history is sickness. Its entire content is a closing of the wound, a winning back of inner meaning, a restoring of bonds, a making whole of that which is incomplete. No longer does any movement occur in unbroken beauty out of its own inner meaning; like an open, outstretched hand, every gesture seems to be awaiting something. No longer is any form complete. Now the world is whole only in that completion which she seeks, in her consummation beyond time. But history itself is eruption and trembles in fever.

This is the intention of our design: to represent the open, injured, bleeding form of this earth, her wounded heart. This plan shows the breached world. Here the people are constituted in the undisguised form of their history. Through this building they confess the "openness" of their situation before the eternal. Everyday life can be deceptive. Home and vocation, the little joys and the portion of our daily lot—these easily awaken the impression that the form of this life is closed and complete in itself. The people tread solemnly out of their daily life into the revealed and primal form of their history, and they find that it is this very same form which inwardly moulds the life of every day. In this interim, filled with the throes of the dying earth and of the coming eternity, they see that their own peculiar task lies in confessing their own inadequacy ever and again until the end, and in fulfilling the law of earth to the very last. As they stand in the darkness within the closed world, they see that their task is to hold out in time as long as it may last, to look to the Light and to the Open and to lead their lives ever in the face of these.

But the structure shows something else, also: it shows that wherever the earthly form breaks off prematurely, God begins; it shows that it is a good and lucid power which prevents the fulfillment of the earth's meaning, that it was through God that the earth was wounded, and that it is the open place in the binding rings which is the sacred place; and finally, it shows that all things are made perfect in God, that in him all things are redeemed, that it is he who makes the earth whole. This plan makes it clear that when emptiness breaks into a thing, God is near, for this invasion of emptiness is not meaningless annihiliation: it is the beginning of growth into the light.

When the people come from their worldly ties to enter this church, they experience their historical form as the form of ministering grace—for even the open and wounded form of this world is sacredly intended, sacredly preserved. Were it not continually nourished, it would have long since exhausted itself. Out from their rearward boundary, earth and space are being constantly renewed; and the world which was on the point of dissolution comes back out of the infinite as abundant light. This great light fills the open vessel and grants it from within the gift of form and radiance. Creation is renewed from its outermost limits and thus the form is preserved.

This happens in the following way:

At first the people arrange themselves around the altar in the open ring and look to the center. In their very ordering itself they forego the bond of inwardness. Then the priest goes forward to the altar as the representative of the people; there he stands erect facing the east, pushed to the boundary of the earth, the last man. And then, across the altar, that is to say across the holy earth with all her gifts, he begins to invoke the Father, to praise him and to beseech him. In the priest, the congregation and Christ within it, face across the earth into the openness. They go to the innermost brink of the world to the place where her shore curves in an open arc about the eternal. The congregation goes to the threshhold of its house and calls out into God's eternity. The holy doctors have always compared this moment with the image in the Song of Songs where the bride steps into the doorway of her home to await the bridegroom. The people are borne forward through the priest as they step to the threshhold and then "look out into the distance." They pour themselves out in the invocation of God and surrender themselves into the infinite direction. This surrender is the third thing; then everything is still. Men have invoked the Creator and they await his answer. The earth is breached and empty. The fourth thing is the answer which God bestows from out of his remoteness. It comes back as streaming light out of the direction into which the people have surrendered themselves. Thence the Word is sent anew into the universe. The light falls upon the altar, thence to stream out into the interior. Now the figure turns around and comes back once more. The priest becomes the ministrant through whom the Word is communicated. In the consummate answer the new form of grace is given as the sacred form of new history. The people are dismissed back into the world, Christ blesses the earth, and, bowing over her in thanks, he turns to face the sacred source. The earth grows new as spiritual land. The annihilation is outweighed by the infinite influx of grace. And the form is preserved, if only by the miracle that it lives not by "bread" but by the Word out of the "mouth" of the heavenly Father.

This very form is like a mighty bird, like an eagle hovering motionless in the sunlight on widespread wings. On beautiful days we may find such examples in nature or we may find them in art—on the architraves of the

Egyptian temples, for example, where a falcon with widespread wings is depicted. Or we may be reminded of the sun, and the way it penetrates and absorbs the clouds with its rays.

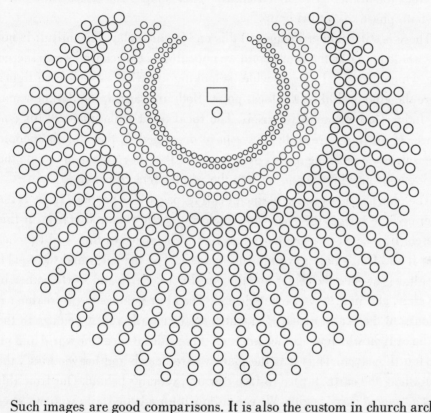

Such images are good comparisons. It is also the custom in church architecture to speak of the "wings" of the building, meaning the transepts which jut out on each side of the altar. And this is indeed justified, just as in another connection we may call the great, longitudinal space a "nave" or "ship."* These spaces really are like "wings" on which the congregation hovers in the light.

We could also speak, with real meaning, of the "tree" of the church and in this plan we find laws of form similar to those which govern the growth

* In Latin "navis" means "ship"; in German "Schiff" means both "nave" and "ship." Tr.

of the trees. Thus the center axis is like the trunk and the people are like the limbs which grow upward and outward simultaneously. But it would be more correct to compare this form to a branch since the tree grows vertically whereas the branch grows horizontally. This comparison stresses the intermediate phase of "growing up."

There is still another image and this one is particularly beautiful. Is not this whole plan like the eye? Could we not call this church God's own sacred eye, which, dark and opened wide, is looking into God's own sacred light? Here the altar would be the focal point. Both are sacred, the darkness and the light: God encounters himself. The focal point is the place of his embrace. If all this were to be as we have described it, then for the people themselves the meaning of this plan would be that they are taken up into the dark eye of providence and up into the resplendent response.

The plan has now been explained in all its parts. The people's space is the intermediate space, the space in which the earthly church stands in this present life, between providence and light. The space of this world arches over it and God's holy government bounds it. For the earth and the world, the altar is at once the center and the threshhold. Earth and world gather in the altar, and in it they reach their end. The altar belongs to two realms: it belongs to the realm of earth in which we can walk and it belongs to the realm of light which we cannot enter, on three sides it faces the world and on the fourth heaven. Thus it is the place where "earth and heaven kiss," the spot where the earth, turned to face eternity, remains behind. Out from this spot a "sacred way" begins. We can follow it for a little while with our eyes but our feet cannot tread it: it runs its course on beyond the universe. As that way which ran from door to altar, this sacred way was already hinted at and already set out upon in the first plan. The way was begun by the priest who trod it, and through him the direction of its course into the eternal was determined. At the point where the centric movement veers out into the infinite stands the impassable portal of heaven: window, threshhold, shining negation, the piercing of the world—and, seen from the world, the shining void, God's other dwelling.

God's radiant dwelling is at the same time his heaven and this is Christ's truer home. The Lord and the Saints have entered into it, they have entered into the light. And thus our everyday situation is not exactly like that of the last supper before the Lord's death. The Lord is with us; Christ lives in the people, he sits with them at table and in their name he speaks with the Father. It is the Lord in the people who goes to the brink of the earth and looks out into the far distance. But in very fact he is no longer present; he is "at the right hand of the Father" in heaven and thence he comes across the threshhold to the earth. Our supper is the true Lord's supper, and yet at the same time it is only its "commemoration." The Lord himself indicated that this was so when he said that he would no longer celebrate this supper on earth, but that he would indeed celebrate it in eternity. And the Apostle, too, indicates this when he says that through the celebration we should proclaim the death of the Lord "until he comes." And thus the empty side is also Christ's empty seat at the table of this world. The death of the Lord and his going forth are the wound where history bleeds. When the Lord departed, he left the world open behind him.

REPRESENTING HEAVEN

On this side of the altar lies the "world." Earth spreads out, men inhabit it, space arches over it and a firmament girdles the universe. In the "openness" beyond the altar lies the "other world," heaven. The altar is the border between time and eternity, "threshhold."

That part of the building which stands for the "world" lies on this side and is the space in which we live. Here we are born, here we may move, here we may work. This part of the building alone can be represented with the means of our art. Everything which it shelters is entrusted to us. Here the architect is at home and on this, his "worldly" task, he may practice the calling he has learned.

Yet even this part of the building is "world" in the true sense of the term —world innocently at play with herself, at rest in her own center of gravity

and in her own graceful motion. In this sense the artist finds no "worldly"
task here either. It is not enough for him to create this part of the building
as a "cosmic analogy" for here the world is standing in prayer. She stands
before the infinite gap and looks to the other side, surrendering herself and
awaiting grace. This world has undergone the great transformation. Her
center of gravity has moved out into the eternal and all her forms are open.
This world is a lesser world than the world outside before the door, it is
poorer and emptier of meaning—and at the same time it is far more. This
building is true world, but it is world in the situation on the threshhold,
world which stands at first in expectancy and which is afterward blessed:
world in prayer. Hence what the artist has here to achieve is "work which
prays"—indeed a genuine likeness of the world, but of a world which is open
to God, and the forms which correspond to this world are the "open forms."
These forms are prayers. They stand open ready to receive the Lord, and in
each of them is "threshhold" and "emptiness." Nor do we learn this kind
of work in the schools as they are today. But this work must be possible,
even as it must be possible for every man to pray, not out of his own power
but because the Creator has given him this. This particular art brings the
world to her own most intrinsic form and then translates her into prayer.

The artists must even be able to achieve the images of the saints: the
images as they are when they stand round about in the "worldly space" along
the walls and on the small altars. It is true that the saints are now in the
eternal light and that we do not know what befell their form when it crossed
the threshhold. Turning utterly to face the eternal vision, this form has
become the answer to God's countenance. But for earthly eyes its outward
appearance is a mystery and hence art cannot tell it.

But the saint who comes back across the threshhold assumes the earthly
form once more since he comes to earth to speak with men. We are told that
when God sends his messengers to men, he lends them a human form
since of themselves they possess no body. He gives them the form which he
designed in speech and response between men. All the pictures which depict
the saints and angels who come from heaven across the threshhold to man

are earthly pictures. The good painter can render them, for it suffices if he shows man—any man—as a creature and in innocence. The painter lives on this side, in the open world, and the open form is appropriate to him. His pictures should be open, they should interrupt the cohesive continuity and open up the way out of it, in order that, through the pictures, faith may find the way to God. The openness of the sacred images is of course different from the openness of earthly creatures in prayer. The latter are empty and await grace whereas the former depend inwardly on the light—they are its re- motest outpost on the earth and their human silhouette is the expression of the light as it enters the world. The painter can sketch the outline. But be- hind it lies the "threshhold": the silhouette itself is threshhold, the light must be given by God.

All that lies on this side, in the worldly space, can be painted by the painter, built by the builder. They can even plan the threshhold and the window which opens into heaven—but then their art is at an end: they can- not enter the other world.

Our churches are not built by angels from heaven. They are built by liv- ing men who themselves stand at a particular point in their own design; and this point lies on this side of the altar, in the midst of mankind. There is no such thing as an absolute architecture, and this is because the great premise of all building is the architect himself, a mortal man to whom heaven is barred. How should he build in a region which he may not enter?

Here there is a gaping hole in the building, but this is neither door nor window as in other structures. Behind other doors lies a new room or a garden or the open out-of-doors. But this gap is absolute opening, the ulti- mate rending, "nothing" more lies behind it: here God's solitude begins. None but those whom he sends from the other side may cross over here. The window, as used by natural architecture, is based on the structure of the eye. The eye is hollow concavity and opening, and in it man opens himself to the world. But through this same eye man closes the outer world once more, rounding it about himself. The eye opens the world and terminates the world, and in this way it produces an elementary architecture. No human eye, however, penetrates the eternal gap, for to see means to gain access, yet the way through this radiant breach is impassable. God's eye follows this path and Christ sees so, but here the human eye does not see. The eye sees with Christ, in faith, yet it does not "really" see—not in this present life.

Here architecture is found wanting. From its own standpoint it would have to close this rift which it has opened. But it is just this which architecture may not do. For this window, this gateway is the eternal rift at the edge of the world and may not close.

Thus this task is insoluble. And still it would be false to reject it because it is not architecturally posed. With equal right, or rather lack of right, we could reject life itself as incapable of form, since at every instant it is subject to this same eternal injunction. Yet nevertheless, in fact for this very reason, life must be lived, and indeed it must be lived in such a way as to be obedient to this injunction. Man's theological situation cannot be formed, we are never finished with it. And yet this very insolubility is here our architectural task. The flight into some sort of classical restraint, into some sort of mellow resignation, is no longer enough. Here no illusion, no officiousness about serving imagined purposes can help us. Here we must confess. Only that architecture is valid here which takes the eternal rift up into its work and which openly admits that here it is found wanting. In doing this art itself becomes "open" like every other creature. The great and valid works all stand before the countenance of the impossible, all were begun in the face of it: mighty approaches to the insoluble solution. Their greatness lies not in their being somehow aesthetically pleasing but rather in their creative assertion of the absolute impossibility, in the fact that each of their forms opens the eternal gap. Perhaps in this one single instance it is truly permissible to separate habitable structure from structure which is symbolical, to end the former at the threshhold and to continue the latter on beyond it. In this case we would close the gap in some imperfect way, using a substance which provides protection against the weather and which at the same time bars our passage—we could make this closing wall transparent, thus enabling us to see out, as it were, onto the symbolical part of the building lying beyond. For indeed, we can convey what lies behind this window only by allusion, by indication. To "indicate" a road means to point it out, to introduce it by intimation without traversing it: the pointing movement itself remains this side of the threshhold.

We could attempt to continue the sacred way symbolically and as a promise. For instance we could make the "window" into a great archway and construct behind it a series of arches of ever-decreasing diameter. The final one would be but a point and thus this "way" would lead through ever remoter archways out into the far, far distance. Naturally this would be an illusion of perspective. But here illusion could be permitted: this "way" would not pretend to be more than an image produced with architectural means. The Baroque builders worked in this manner.

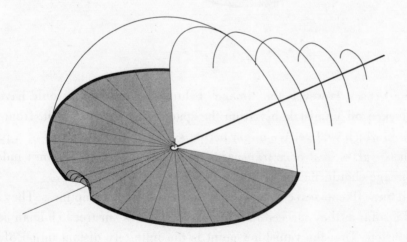

Or we could attempt to render the infinite through the windings and intertwinings of a "fluid" space in the manner of some of the medieval cathedrals: ever and again a new egress opens up—the whole structure is lost in the incalculable.

By continuing the way on out to the horizontal edge of the world we could even draw nature into this likeness. This would be possible where the window opens onto an empty landscape, which then lies between the threshhold and the horizon, for example on the shore of the ocean or at the edge of the desert or on a high mountain top.

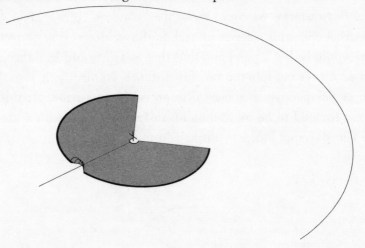

In all cases, however, the "image" behind the threshhold would have to be blocked off unmistakably from the space lying in front of it, from the space in which we live. We might perhaps achieve this by means of a pane of glass—glass is at once transparent and hard—or by a grating: indeed this image should mean "pathway which we cannot tread."

All these likenesses seek to say that God dwells in the emptiness. They are good insofar as they succeed in bringing "emptiness" nearer to human comprehension. That the vanishing point is the infinitely distant union of all parallel ways, that the paths of the labyrinth intertwine endlessly, that the horizon flees before us: all these things can be likenesses, likenesses of the fact that the place where God dwells in solitude does not lie in this world, that where he dwells is the "silent waste" which no earthly foot has trod and into which no path of this world leads. These likenesses seek to say, further, that our world is at once closed in itself and yet open to God. In the natural sense it ends within itself and in the spiritual sense it is open.

These images are good in what they lack—they can help the world to renounce herself. But we may easily misunderstand what they say. When these plans join onto the habitable space a second space to which—although we may not enter it—our eyes and our thoughts and all the subtler powers of the soul have access, then all this may be rightly understood as an image of the "spiritual" openness of the eternal gap. But we can also draw from this the erroneous conclusion that God's dwelling lies infinitely far away and that he who wishes to go to him must cross over "the wastes of the universe," purifying his soul and leaving the body ever farther behind, until finally, at the very end, even of the inaccessible itself, he may enter in before the countenance of God. For some, this may be a way of symbolically realizing the holy negation: it may be for them a route, or a detour to God, but such asceticism is not the legitimate way. The sacred void, this resplendent abundance, begins at the very heart of the world, at the spot where the rift has forced its farthest tip to the world's innermost brink: here the final gap begins, here, in the midst of the world, is the place of sacrifice.

Even worse would be the error of mistaking the inaccessible part of the world for God's dwelling place and the forms of abstraction for God's form. Men have often fallen victim to this error.

In the end all earthly movements lead out of the narrow, friendly area which is the lot of human life, out of the area in which alone it is lasting: the movement of thought leads into the cold laws of logic, that of research into the wastes of the stars and the atoms, that of contemplation to the brink of the void, the movement of art into the great and uninhabitable forms; all end at last in the trackless waste.

Man cannot exist there for he needs the air and the fruits of the earth. And yet a profound wisdom tells him that his spirit has its home there outside. An unquenchable longing drives him into the great law. On the high mountain peaks, at the edge of the deserts, under the starry firmament, a stirring of true human greatness awakes in him. And in the face of death he builds his cathedrals of a spirit grown free, his arrogant machines, his structures of pure calculation. (In the Freiburg spire we may experience what truly exalted architecture is: great mathematical forms standing open under the heavens, raged through by the storms, granting no shelter to men.)

Man's longing for the stars is good when it stays within its proper human realm. It should be for him a likeness of the yearning for his eternal home. His ascent to the great structures of the mind should encourage him for the greater ascent to God, and the uninhabitableness of these forms should remind him of the inaccessibleness of the "other world."

But he must not confuse likeness with reality for here the world lures him with her most potent temptation, the temptation of the Titans. She seeks to entice him out into the great structures, where, set down in the trackless universe, he is destroyed. She tells him that the titanic felicity is eternal bliss, that the abstract is divine, that God himself is the great calculator, and that works, purified to number, are sacred image, that God is the wasteland and his dwelling the inaccessible.

All this is nothing but world in its highest exaltation—we mean this without the least bitterness—great and sublime, yet temporal image. Its legitimate place lies not behind the gap but here on this side, within the universe, between our heads and the vault. The movement into the heights is something very great—the cathedrals of the mind are glorious. We should not be suspicious of them nor revile them. God did not wish men mildly modest and "moderate": he wished them bold. But these things remain a likeness, and even the fruitful earth is a likeness too.

But in the end God is utterly different. And while the ascetic is scaling the lonely peaks perhaps God is in the valley, playing with the children and the flowers.

In order to avoid all these errors it might be best not to work out the image at all but instead to leave the structure with the rift in it. The open place would simply remain empty, a meaningful break in the ring. This could be intimated by leaving a part of the wall behind the altar utterly white. White is the abundance of all the colors, the unalloyed and complete light; and at

the same time it is the negation of all colors, for it is itself no longer a color:
it transcends them all. In this it is like the void of the mystic which is in truth
the infinite fullness. Here we may by no means place the altar directly
against the wall, as is so often done today out of scanty reflection, nor may
its emptiness be concealed with something or other (for then it becomes for
the first time truly and completely empty, that is to say void.) We must be
aware that the wall which remains empty here has something significant of
its own to say, that it is not the termination of the altar but rather its un-
locking and opening, and that for the whole building, too, it represents
something utterly different from a simple back wall.

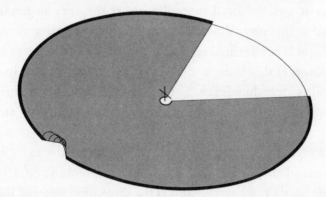

Or we can go one step further back and retain heaven completely within
this world; we limit ourselves to the latter, but form it in the way in which
it borders on the Beyond. We show only what lies on this side, nothing more:
we render the coastline of this earth. It forms a great arc of shoreline yet the
sea within it does not belong to it. But if we pursue the course of this coastline and draw it in—indeed, it is also the contour of the Beyond—we gain
some understanding of the power which cuts this fjord in the land. Heaven
becomes visible as effect.

Here we show the community in the wide-open ring and the single individual as he steps to the center and turns to face into the openness. This,
also, is an intimation. As a ray, man's eye forces its way into the distance
but this same eye is also the pool into which the distance falls. It is his body's

charge to go further; but he can also stop and stand quietly. When he stands, his standing is not like that of a mountain or a tower—it is rather an expectant awaiting which calls on the far distance asking it to come to him; and the more quietly he waits the more surely does it come. With his voice he makes himself audible afar off. But his voice is also the means of speech for him and in each spoken word is already contained the beginning of a discourse and the plea for reply. When man, standing in quiet expectation, turns to God and speaks out his holy name, the answer comes back to him out of the remote distance.

Thus the simple standing of the people in the open ring is itself the intimation, for it was the Lord himself who, at the very beginning, taught them to stand in this way. When the people follow him they sit with him at table. This form is not the final one but it precedes the final form as question precedes answer. If this form of the world is still empty, then its emptiness says that God is rich abundance, when it is dark, it makes manifest his sacred light, when it is open, it awaits him as its consummation and completion.

Is not the church, when she so stands, like one of the early sculptured figures who stand in prayer with upraised arms, embracing a space—the space of their heads and hearts—and at the same time uttering the heartfelt plea that God may come? And is not the whole of mankind standing like this before the Lord in the earthly interim?

Here we would not go beyond a provisional closing of the east side. The space looses itself somehow out toward the east; what lies beyond finds no expression; this part of the building has no significance, it gives no testimony, the whole pointing movement, the whole "intimation" is taken back into the people themselves. This may be interpreted to mean that the movement of surrender has already been brought to an end and that at this instant the opposite movement begins. The "moment on the threshhold" has become form: that instant when a movement is about to reverse itself—that moment pregnant with hidden decision, whose apparent stillness is the second of silence in the center of history. There is a sort of simple standing which possesses great historical meaning. The artists of antiquity already held the instant when time stands still to be the faithful inspiration of their "statues" (from the Latin "statuere" = "to stand" Tr.). But there is a difference—the classical situation was greatest concentration of historical power, whereas this Christian instant is consummate powerlessness. Before the eternal, the Christian is strongest when nothing more is left him. At this moment neither earth nor heaven exists, the borderline blurs, there is no longer a boundary to the earth, and therefore any ending of its space beyond the most provisional would be meaningless. The emptiness has in this instant reached the people themselves. They have become the "place" where it is represented, and that which is represented is the mysterious *status nascendi* of grace.

We would like to describe one final possible design for the eastern part of the building:

In this design the window is once more fully built out and behind it, flooded with light, lies a broad, domed space. This space is utterly empty and utterly white.

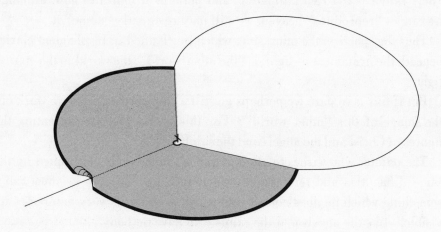

This plan is distinguished from all previous ones in that it transcends the statement that God lives in "emptiness," that this place is "inaccessible,"

that toward this "emptiness" the world is "open," that there negation befalls all worldly forms. The previous proposals were intended to introduce
and to ease the negating movement. But here an assertion is made, the
assertion that the other world also has a form which, when transposed into
its opposite, corresponds to the form of this world. The world's dark outline
is turned to lightness and a vaulting of light replies to her night-firmament.

Seen naturally, this design is presumptuous, it violates the eternal boundary. What makes us consider it and what perhaps also justifies it does not
come from the natural possibilities of art—heaven is barred to art—but
from revelation. We offer the idea, at least as a question, and we ask
whether, in the prayer which the Lord taught us to pray: "Father who art in
heaven," there does not lie a sort of injunction to represent this heaven.
This prayer is not simply the "no" to the world and her form—above and
beyond this it is a revelation which reveals God's form to be a fatherly one.
But again this is not an actual representation. That which is given us so
understandably in the word "Father" is taken from us again by the addi-
tional statement that he is in another place. This is neither a "yes" nor a
"no," rather is it a rich intimation, and perhaps it indicates how, although
we cannot "reproduce" heaven, we still may reverently "name" it.

Thus the space on the other side, which lies bathed in resplendent clarity
beneath the firmament of light, is "the other world," the world in the eternal
light.

But if this is so dare we perhaps go still a step further, dare we work out
the image of this "other world"? For this would mean representing the
figures of Christ and the angels and the saints.

The painter who wishes to attempt this is immediately confronted by the
same difficulties and temptations which face the builder: he must paint
something which he does not see and which even by its very nature is "invisible," like the angels and the saints who have no body.

Usually when the painters are confronted with this task they confuse this
world with the next. In this world their task is to show man as he really is.
But what is he like, really? He is not as we encounter him every day—in

truth he is otherwise. Some think he is more spiritual and they try to render figures of fervent ardour. Others think he is more timeless: the historical accident is but a test and a passage, that with which man is charged and the things which befall him, these are not man himself, these he must overcome; his true being is ever the same and has no history. (On the graves of antiquity we already find the soul in a youth which never ages.) Others think that man is possessed of a more lawful nature and they discover measure in him. Still others believe that it is *within* the historical matrix that the essential is to be found, and they render the outward form with painful exactitude. In one way or other all are right, and all agree in saying that the image of man is not automatically given and that to represent him truly is not easy. It may happen that someone, as he watches man and ponders him, suddenly recognizes in him the creature. This experience can be so sacred for him who sees that he thinks he has caught sight of heaven. This is the most beautiful of all errors but even so only an error.

All the many transformations which art may undertake with the world remain *in* this world; they may interpret the things or spoil them, at best they are a likeness of the great transformation. But heaven is not a collection of geometrical figures. Man, as God meant him, has a destiny which changes him. The saints never lose their wounds nor do they become children again; what they have done and suffered is theirs for eternity. Heaven does not restore the purity of original creation: it terminates destiny and it shows that this destiny was intended and sent. Neither the insides nor the outsides of the things are of heaven. Only a very few processes of the artistic transformation lead up to the very threshhold and not one of them crosses over it. God alone can achieve this, art cannot. If we possessed only art, the place beyond the threshhold would have to remain empty. The real question begins only when art has done its work. For after having discovered man as the Creator intended him, art would have to lead men into the eternal vision, and this she cannot do.

But perhaps, empowered only by the tidings about the fatherliness of the eternal, we can, through the images, "name" what lies beyond, instead of trying to reproduce it. Perhaps we may achieve this if we give, as it were, a silhouette of the sacred. A transparent representation can reveal in a most meaningful way. The great drawn forms then become at every point horizons, and in their infinite vista that which is intended becomes visible: the creatures bathed in the light of God.

Perhaps the mosaics in the choirs of the early churches were conceived in this way. The apsis represents a spiritual horizon filled with the gold of the heavenly light and in it the holy figures appear. They are bathed in God's golden effulgence. At that time people knew very well, and the church councils also established, that the images are illusions and that the reverence shown them "passes over" to their prototype. And so these representations are, as it were, gates of heaven: through their outlines we see eternity. The likeness of heaven became shining and translucent in fact when the walls of the choirs vanished and their place was taken by the stained glass windows. The sunlight shone through them and in them it took on color. Conversely the golden figures on the wings of the altars glistened more in the candle light. In them the apse returned once more. The concave sweep of the apse points into the distance, out of the apse the church shines like a radiant star. But this same apse embraces and shelters—it is the image of the distant heaven but also of its imminent approach. Apse, altar wall and chalice are the steps on which heaven descends.

All these images stand directly on the threshhold. They fill the windows with colors and outlines through which the sun shines in. Transient forms are these, heaven on the point of entering the world or world on the point of leaving the earth. No mortal eye has seen what happens beyond them.

But the success of such a representation is not a question of artistic method. Great talent can even be a danger here. The building and the imagery may be modest, shabby, even executed without skill. This is too bad but it is not decisive. Truly decisive is, that the peculiar act of reverent "naming" succeed.

Sacred Parting

The Chalice of Light

THIS PLAN, too, shows the world in leave-taking. The world lies open under heaven. The people stand in a ring about the altar, the sacrifice of their prayers rises "like incense" and the eternal Word descends. The

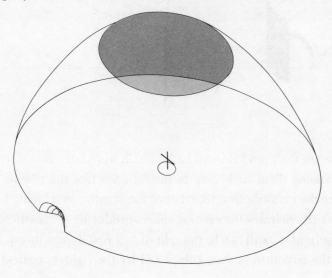

"open heaven" comes down to the altar to dwell in the midst of men.

There are many beautiful examples of this architectural form. Already in very early times we find the domed buildings of Mycaenae whose vaults, set directly on the ground, lead in a single great sweep from the circular base to the round opening in the dome. High above we see out into the universe: architecture has been left out in favor of nature. But this is a nature from which, through the use of the "cleft," all nearness and all warmth of life have been removed; all that remains of nature is the remote and lofty law of infinite space and its constellations.

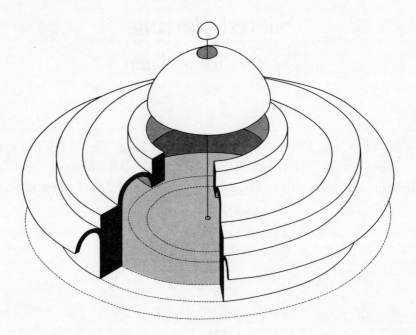

Then there are the round Roman baths which were later transformed into baptistries, among them such very beautiful ones like the one in Brescia. And there are the mausoleums, like that of Constantia, in which a half-dark cylindrical vault encircles the central space, producing a "basilical" cross-section. This circular vault can be thought of as a first dome: its top has been cut out and the structure is then completed by the lighter, central cupola.

When complete, the architectural solution always consists of two domes built one into the other, the window in the crown of the dark dome below being closed by the lighted dome above. Usually a ring of windows breaks through the foot of the upper dome to illumine it. The dome seems to hang in mid-air above an open cave, set free from the earth by a ring of light. The dome of the Santa Sophia in Byzantium is constructed in this way.

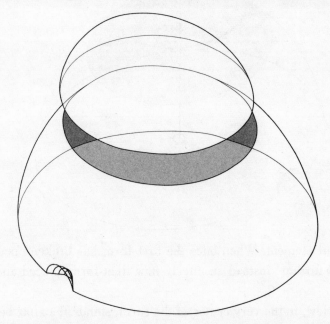

In the Baroque this idea was highly developed through the use of painting. Ever and again one open dome is set above the other until finally this vertical heavenly perspective ends in utter light.

The basic conception of all these solutions is alike. Each time a circle is cut out of the crown of the dome and each time this window is the source of light for the space beneath. In the one case it is the universe which closes the structure, spanning over it the vault of the heavens and thus placing a second dome of infinite diameter over the first. Another time a constructed dome completes the space, not, however, by continuing it and closing it but rather by adjoining it as a cope of light. And this second dome is a completely new

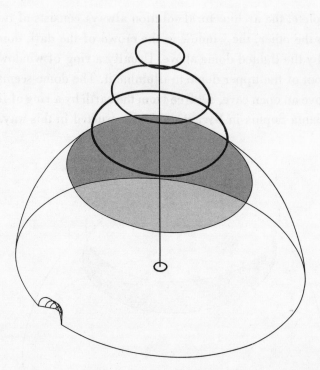

architectural element. When once the first form has broken open it is not carried out further: instead an utterly new light-form, placed above it, replies to it.

Down below, in the very center of the earth, stands the altar beneath the open heavens. Through the altar the earth rises up toward the light; steps emphasize the ascent and the people stand round about in the same ordering as in the first plan, looking to the center. From the dome a ray of light falls into the darkness illumining within it the altar. The altar passes on the light like the things onto which a ray of sunlight falls. The altar itself is not sun but illumined earth, neither star nor seed, but "eye," which is to say: world which sees the sun.

The spot on which the altar stands belongs simultaneously to two worlds. For the ground and its ordering this place is the center; the people, standing in rings around it, look to the earth's brightest spot. And thus in all things which concern the earth it is the star-image which rules. But this spot is not bright of itself—it transmits light but it produces none. It receives the light before the rest of the earth and in greater fullness. But this light comes to it from above and thus it lives from this "above" as from another world, a world which is more radiant than the earth and whose gift to the earth is the light. This place is open to the heavens, it consorts with the things which are there and transmits them to the earth. This center is like an open chalice. In the center the whole building is already at hand, for this entire structure is itself like a chalice for the light. From the very inside to the very outside the chalice-form pervades the whole.

This plan unites elements of the first and second designs. If we consider the ground-plan alone, we find not the slightest change from the first plan. Buildings of this type have therefore often been called "centric" although in reality they are so only in regard to their horizontal ordering. If we consider the cross-section alone we find it so similar to the ground-plan of the second design that we are tempted to think of these two as variants of the same basic figure, as variants which may easily be carried over into one another. If the second plan were to be turned on edge so that the windows were on top, then the sphere, which the influence of gravity had pressed flat to the circular base, would round out once more and the window would become circular. At the same time that part of the figure which would then be at the bottom would be pressed against the earth. But for the rest, the figure would remain undamaged. Even the different ways of building the radiant parts could be retained. They are found in both plans in exactly corresponding form: as shining vaulting, as completing firmament, as a perspective of open domes and so on. But where two figures correspond so exactly, we would also expect to find the same meaning.

Geometrically speaking this would be correct. But architecture is not geometry. It is the forming of our own destiny. We cannot turn its plans this way and that and look at them from above and from the outside, for we are ourselves worked into them. We ourselves, our own life, our soil, our people, God as he is to us here and now—that is what these plans are.

The theme of the former design was the ultimate homelessness of man, of man who needs the confines and yet relinquishes them, of him whom life's gentle commandment keeps to the ring of the community and the little garden of home, and who yet opens the circle because another commandment points him out of its confines and because he knows that he has "been sent on the way." But here in this plan we are concerned with man's "uprising." This plan owes its existence to the contradiction which man raises to gravity when he meets the burden of its downward pull with an easing, upward movement. This movement continues on up to the crown of the dome and then pierces it; in this piercing man overcomes his own heaviness, for this vault is formed of heaviness and heaviness pervades it from top to bottom—it is our own destiny: we ourselves are earth.

The subject of this design is the age-old struggle between man and earth. In it, man stands for buoyancy, lightness and clarity against heaviness, darkness, unformedness—for the delicate against the massive. Extricating himself from the earth and her clutches, he renews victoriously the age-old legend.

The first uprising created the body. Its buoyant form contradicts for the first time the dumb heaviness of earth, its tall growth the earth's unfathomable depths. The body stands erect, a contradiction in the midst of space. But in opposition the earth invents the vault. The vaulting overhead is again earth, earth which has closed over anew, burying the body once more in her womb. This is the answer which the body itself provoked by its uprising: the earth turns up her surface to form a vault, her depths become a cave and she clutches the mutineer still tighter, forcing him now into her innermost center. But for the second time he shatters the earthly fetters and frees himself forever into light.

Now man is standing there: he has shattered the cave. Through a great hole its depths flow out and light streams in. Thus he brings fire to the earth. He himself is not light but a torch, and he belongs neither to heaven nor to earth. His feet stand widespread on the ground and his head towers up into the light, from below the dark heaviness of earth flows through him, from above light floods him, and in him the two streams mingle. But despite all his mutiny was meant for the earth—through his conquest he sought to give her her own true form. He makes of her fertile soil.

If the form at the beginning was understood as cave, we understand the new form as landscape. The cave splits open at the crown and the heavens are opened, the sinking sides become a chain of mountains stretching across the horizon. The depths turn to a vale. An open valley lies beneath the sun and it is bordered far in the distance by a remote range of mountains. But in the midst of this sheltered mead rises a high peak. The sunlight falls early upon it. Its summit is already aglow when the first light brushes the mountain tops and the valley still lies in twilight. On its slopes the light slowly sinks until it reaches the bottoms of the valleys and gilds the whole sacred plain.

This is the sacred landscape of olden times:

Opened to a vale and wrought like a chalice, the land lies outspread in quiet expectation, her form opened wide. Man stands erect in the center as mountain. In him the earth has reached her decision, he it was who freed her, giving her the valley-form. In ancient times the pyramid stood in this landscape, the king who is so big that his feet reach to the roots of the earth and his head to the heavens. Here, too, stood the ziggurat, which ascended in layers of color, its golden summit glistening in the early light; and on this highest upland stood an open shrine, within it a lodging made ready for the young, holy light.

The ancient sacred concern for the landscape, for its valleys and mountains and for the things which they bring forth, for everything which sinks its roots into the earth and lifts its head into the light, for all those things which grow tall between heaven and earth and, in partaking of them both, stand beautifully bounded—all of these things are taken over by this plan. The great theme of its prayer is the flourishing of the fruits of the field, the sanctity and the care of growing life. This plan beseeches God to renew life in every day and in every year and to allow it to grow tall in innocence as eternal life. The plan asks this by its existence, by simply standing in holy growth.

It is not an accident that this plan is so similar to that of the great temple of Demeter in Eleusis and that they share the same reverent relationship to light and the same centric ordering of the people. Here as there, life is conceived in its great and universally valid movement. But in Eleusis this happened in the form of a chthonian cult which, in mystic rite, let life itself carry out its own primary movement, and which initiated a peasant folk into it. Here this happens in the form of Christian sacrifice, which offers up the primal movement of life and then receives it back again, now more beautiful, now new creation. The old rite repeated the natural movement through participating in the need and the joy of the sacred earth. It came to the earth's innermost point but did not go beyond it to the ultimate brink where life is ever lifted anew out of nothingness. And thus it did not lead its initiates to yield utterly to the creative omnipotence and so to experience its movement themselves. It led deep down into the roots and then let itself be forced up again by the rising sap. And so it remained a prisoner of life.

The new rite possesses a profounder knowledge of the way the things succeed. It begins absurdly. It inaugurates a movement which repudiates life and it carries it through to the point where both movements cancelling each other end in nothingness, in utter emptiness. For the new rite it is this point of complete powerlessness which is the fruitful moment, the moment in which a truer world goes forth out of the hands of the Creator.

In the finished building the creative process has been stilled to structure. Here the form has reached its final shape and the movement which begot the building flows unnoticeably through it, renewing it ever and again. In order to catch sight of this movement we must go back into the time when the building did not yet exist and then allow it to grow up gradually. Then we see the process of holy consummation, we see how it brings forth one form around the other and how it transforms one into the other, until at last the final form comes into being. Each one of these intermediate forms can be built as an individual church in which all that went before and all that follows is organically contained. The final form harbors all of these churches within itself.

The cave is the first of these sacred forms. Closed is the womb of earth, undelineated her heavy mass. She lies in darkness, sunk deep in dream and night.

In the second form axial paths traverse the earth which then condenses in rings. The land strives to the center and the dark star-image forms—the image under which the earth surrenders herself into her center. Finally she has drawn herself in altogether and is gathered completely in her innermost point.

In the third image the earth rises up out of this densest point and grows into the heights. At first a hill arises in the center, and the altar becomes the sacred mountain which the priest used to climb for the sacrifice; then the movement takes vertical leave of the soil as axis.

The star turns into the flame which climbs high as column—the seed has burst and sends forth a shoot. Just as the oil flows from all sides to the

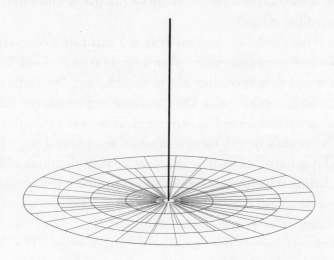

center and then, changed to flame, is consumed as it climbs high, so, too, does the space move, and in climbing it annihilates itself. The people stand around the flame in the ring but in reality they themselves are the fuel.

In the flame men have always seen the image of sacrifice and in a sense this is right, for this form *is* "sacrifice." Yet the comparison is not completely correct. What happens invisibly—the surrender to the center and the ascent from it—is like the movement of the flame. But the earth cannot give more than her darkness and just as the first star was dark and inverted, so the flame of sacrifice is not light but dark. The sacrificial flame thus repudiates the flame of natural fire and when it strikes the crown of the dome an opening is formed through which the fullness of earth quits the cave.

The next form is a chalice: the earth has become utterly concave and lies beneath the heavens like an empty vessel. The gathering and ascending movement is exhausted, the earth has surrendered herself and is now utter hollowness. All is still, waiting in sheer readiness.

The final form shows the answer. In the golden rain of light the dark flame of sacrifice returns, the depths are filled with light, the earth is new once more. The light descends and the image of the natural flame, whose movement climbs, is once again reversed. It can be compared with a darting flame pointed toward the ground.

For the sinking part of the process there is a still better comparison: this is the figure which comes into being when a liquid is poured out, falling in a single stream and then spreading out in rings below. The flame signified: gathering, ascent, annihilation. The "pouring out" contains the falling, striking, piling up and spreading out—it gives answer to the flame. When the stream falls onto a liquid, there is in addition a plowing up, a hollowing out and the breaking of waves in rings. Here we may also think of the figure in which a falling stone disturbs quiet water: at first a trough forms, then concentric waves spread outward from it and then, at the spot where the stone struck, a column of water rises high.

But this comparison is not completely correct either. The forms are similar but in the plan they take a different course: first the dark inverted star forms, then the axis grows out of it and finally the figure flows out over the path which has been prepared for it. This mysterious flame, the form of the earth's dark ecstasy, determines the entire first part of the movement. The image of pouring makes its appearance only when the light enters the figure. It seems as if each natural image undergoes a sacred inversion when it enters the sanctuary, in order that, as a figure which disavows the earth, it may become fit for the divine service: only the answer renews the natural order.

Could we also perhaps understand this sacred disavowal as the first answer to a first movement which, still earlier and in utter secrecy, came from God to be carried out in the world? Perhaps a hidden pre-history, which took place even before the movement of sacrifice began, makes clear everything which later came to pass. In the beginning God shattered the dome and fell like a stone into the waters of earth. Then it was that the earth rose up. To her the image of a new creation rose resplendent like a star, and this shining vision drove her to disavow her natural star-form and to surrender it. Nature senses the better design within herself and led by the presentiment of more beautiful creation she yields herself that she may be created anew: she takes leave of her dwelling and goes forth like a bride to meet the spirit.

Again the sacred mountain forms in the center, now a mountain fraught with grace. Brooks of sacred light flow down into the valley and the spoked wheel is formed of star and ring.

This is then the final form: what is above changes places with what is below, their two streams, mingling, merge to produce a first form of innocent-holy growth. This form is like a tree whose roots reach down into the earth and whose branches reach up into the light, so that it is made up of two parts, one light and the other dark.

We do not mean this externally—the outward form of a tree bears little resemblance to this building. But what a tree is inside, the way it pushes outward from within and the forms which its life assume from within— these things are so. In respect to its inner space, this building is like a mysterious, sacred tree, the epitome of all natural growth. In it the movement of life is redeemed. Up from the center of the landscape this structure grows —it is the holy cathedral of this world and "the birds of the sky nest in it." Thus the sacred world-tree of our forefathers is strangely confirmed—the spiritual tree stands indeed in the middle of the garden. And confirmed, too, is the image of the church which the Lord drew when he called her a tree.

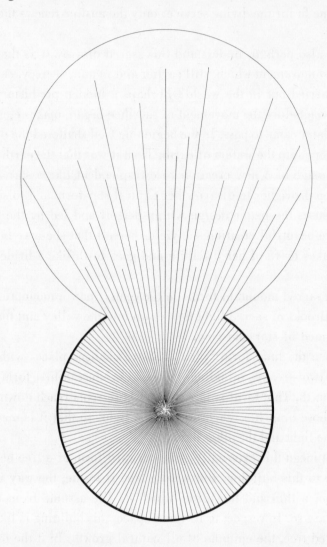

We understand the church tower in the same way. These holy towers, so difficult to explain, which stand overlooking our countryside wherever men have settled in cities and villages, are the solitary, sacred trees of life. It is not as if their task were to illustrate the old concept of the world-tree, but as they stand, full of holy concern, looking out over the countryside, they are pervaded by the same powers which created the ancient concept.

Our plan contains the spoked wheel which unites in itself ring and star, a circling and a centric movement. Through its center passes the axis. Axis and wheel together make up a form-pair which is one of the most important basic figures in the structure of the world. We already discovered it to be the form of the portal—vaulting and gateway—and we drew attention to the solenoid. If we fuse the circling and the axial motions into a single movement the spiral results—a centric movement which simultaneously climbs and circles. All plants grow in accordance with this form—we are tempted to call it the idea of the tree.

In the Bible the form is seldom described and when it is we sense the unmasking of a mystery—as when Stephen sees the "open" heaven or when the prophet climbs the mountain to receive the law in long discourse with God. The Lord rose up at his transfiguration, but this phase was soon over; and also he blessed the earth when he took leave of her—he rose slowly and his own stood "for a long time gazing after him."

This final picture which the Lord left in the memory of his disciples is also the final explanation of this plan. This picture says that this plan is the form in which the church still gazes after the departing Lord. And when he said that he would now go home to the Father he himself elucidated this image still further. This ascent is thus the movement of returning homeward to the Father.

Is this a hint that the theological meaning of the form lies in its being an answer to God's movement? Would all earthly growth then be a likeness of it, and would every motion of the world be embedded ultimately in God's own movement? Would the fact that the world moves at all be understandable only from this starting point? Would the form of all natural growth then receive a theological meaning? The earth herself would be confirmed in this. The earth is the direction whence the movement comes as heaven is the direction whither it flows. And afterward the meaning reverses once again: the earth, too, is God's holy dwelling—holy the dark, heavy readiness of the soil, holy the abyss of her womb in which God rules.

This would make many things simpler for man. His openness, his transiency, his being driven to the heights and to the light—these things would not be a flight from the earth but a reply to God's movement; the same sacred restlessness which drives him to the heights would lead him back once more to the earth. In the midst of light he will long for the darkness, in the midst of the clear and the visible he will long for shelter. And this, too, may be a likeness. To the earth man should remain true, not because he must but because she is sacred earth.

And thus in the end all human movements would possess the same meaning. And at the very last the two forms of the movement of opening would have the same significance. If we understand man in terms of his theological meaning, then the opening movement is the same both times, regardless of whether it seeks its way out forward or upward.

Be all that as it may, for the present the two movements remain differentiated and we shall not try to decide how far such speculations might carry. We leave the two plans side by side, each in its own particular way legitimate structure of sacred world.

The temptation of earth, too, appears in the life of the Lord, the temptation of beginning the movement autonomously instead of sacredly—and the mockery in which such attempting ends: the blackness implicit in the darkness, the hell implicit in the cave. The devil leads the Lord onto a high mountain top and the valley is the temptation which he spreads out before him. And then later on he raises him on the cross and the darkness claps together overhead.

All this provides still another clue for working out that part of the building which represents the "open." What would have to be said here corresponds closely to what has already been said about the representation of heaven and hence it need not be repeated. Here, too, we find the belief that God's holy dwelling begins at an outermost edge of the world. Age-old cosmologies provide us with the images: a firmament of fire spans the universe and the throne of the Almighty stands at its apex. Prayers rise like clouds of incense up to this highest throne and, from above, grace descends. Today it is no longer as easy as it was a half a century ago to mock such a world-image: to us that world in which we build and serve God has ceased to be astronomical theory and has become simply "world for us." In this world the highest light *is* in the zenith and the sun possesses a spiritual meaning. Therefore it is meaningful to recognize in the cope above our heads the firmament of heaven.

We must make one qualification. The statement that "God is above" holds true for only a few of the forms which the process assumes. At the beginning it seems as if God were in the middle—indeed, this is what moves the earth to surrender herself into the center; and then his dwelling transfers itself into the heights, drawing the world up after it. Here heaven lies at the finest tip of the climbing flame; then the rain of light streams down from above. Before and afterward there is a short instant when it seems as if God dwells on the mountain top, and in the very middle of the process he dwells in "emptiness"—in that which is within the chalice, in the space which the walls bound and which upward has no end, which is empty at the beginning and afterward of infinite fullness. Here the altar is his holy throne: his dwelling reaches down to the very slab of the table. Here, too, we could say that God is above; it would be more correct to say: "he is here, his throne stands in the midst of the world." At the very end there is still another place where God dwells. Here we find that form which is built of his very presence, filled to overflowing with it, the form in which his sacred darkness climbs upward and his sacred light flows down into the very roots. "God is present" would be the right word for this final state. Infinite holiness fills this innocent young creature, and in it heaven dwells. Here, too, there is a remnant of the assertion that God is "above"—it no longer designates a place in the "beyond" but rather the movement in which the sacred stance is constantly taking form.

This plan is seldom to be met with in Christian art.

The tradition of genuine centric building was alive in the east when Christian art began. The domes of Mycaenae are a part of it. The Christians took over this tradition, yet they overcame it when they opened the encircling periphery by means of the apse: the altar was not placed below the center of the dome but rather removed to the periphery. There it belongs at the same time to the central space beneath the dome and to the apsidial space at the horizon. The circular space has become the space for the people. It is intersected by the eyes as they look to the altar and also by the pathway which leads from doorway to apsis. Thus it is no longer at rest within itself but has become a station on the way—now it is only one phase and no longer the center.

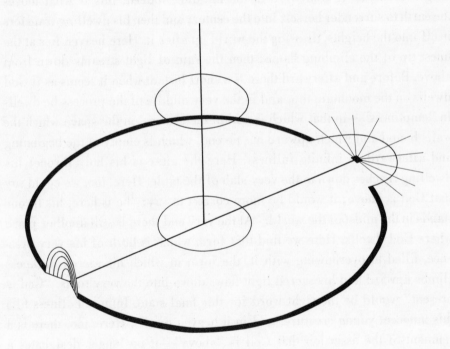

These churches are not genuine centric structures. To be more correct we would have to call them obstructed rectangular structures: the centric form which they inherited is contradicted by the displaced position of the altar. The altar is something which stands at the edge and protrudes from the circular space. The life and the form of the structure do not coincide.

As has already been shown, these buildings are opened simultaneously forward and upward and thus they join two movements in dissonant form. As they stand, they are not consummate works. Their tensions intersect one another: the upward, thrusting movement emerges from a space which is only an intermediate one in relation to the pathway from door to altar; and this path itself ends in a small and unimportant niche which adjoins the space below the dome. If we consider everything very exactly, we find that in these buildings we must in fact assume two dwelling places of heaven, and this is impossible. Indeed the technical means of the time were still too limited to bring the two to unity.

The other form of the opening, in which the opening movement runs its course vertically, as in our third plan, has only rarely been used for churches. Perhaps it is not good to reveal life's most intrinsic and intimate movement—indeed, the natural world, too, lives primarily on the horizontal; that second movement which crosses through all this, the movement of lifting, the erect growth, the overcoming of gravity, this is the accompaniment to all life, a concomitant conquest pervading everything which stands. In the standing of the walls and in the growth of archways and vaulting the vertical movement flows through the churches, too; and wherever there is a sacred picture or a sacred statue it is depicted. This form is almost always to be found in baptistries and mausoleums. Burial and baptism are movements into the depths: the dead are let down into the womb of the earth, in the dome the earth closes over the grave for a second time, and the light high above gives promise of the resurrection. He who is baptised is lowered into the waters and this, too, is a sort of interment. Only the places where the human being is lowered into the earth and where he goes forth out of it were enchased in the works of sacred architecture—only in these two cases did the earth become the one single theme. But this theme is not dealt with in our plan: here it is the old theme of the grain of wheat given in its Christian setting.

The case is much the same with the basilica.

Externally, a structure like St. Clemens in Rome is a long hall—and it is in just this that it differs from the hall of law which, indeed, lay close enough as a model. Here the central nave contains only the altar with the choir in front of it and the seats of the priests behind it. The people stood down below in the nave, and later on in the two side aisles, forming in both cases a wide arc about choir and altar. Thus they were rightly spoken of as "circumstantes," "those who stand about."

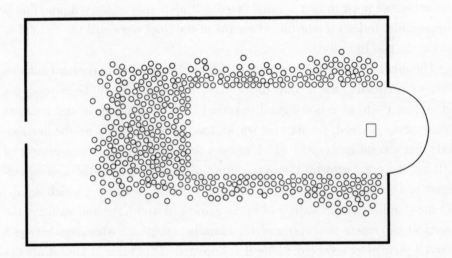

Nor does the life of the building merge with its structural form in the basilica, not even when a transept has been added so that the resulting T-form makes the semi-circle easily recognizable. It seems as if it would have been so simple to pull the side aisle around in the form of a horseshoe and thus show the ordering of the people architecturally. Yet this never happened. The development proceeded differently. At first, "side rooms" for the altar service were built at the ends of the two "side aisles," then "side altars" were built there in special apses and finally real choirs. At that time, in the early Middle Ages, the old spatial unity fell apart into three churches—three churches which ran parallel to each other and were connected by arcades. The Middle Ages saw in them something like sacred worlds whose single districts had little intercourse with one another, or as one realm in which many princes ruled under Christ the King. But in any case the basilica of the early period can be called an obstructed centric structure. In its rectangular structure, just as in the circular structure, an unresolved remnant was left over—some part of the whole was prevented from being fully carried out. Deep within these forms—which were so often simply taken over—the secret form of the Christian church lies hidden. This form is contained neither in the closed comprehensiveness of the dome nor in the long ranging of the nave. Bursting the one and closing the other, she stands between them in a state of inwardness and yet of displacedness, of having and of not having, of sheltering and of summoning.

Sacred Journey
The Way

T HE FOURTH PLAN is sacred journey. This plan completes the parting
and carries out the movement which was made ready in the second
plan. Thus it finishes the second plan. The people's ordering had already
broken apart into the open rings and these now straighten out into the ranks
of an army on the march; the way, which was already secretly present, now
comes out in bold relief; a world which has already ceased to be sheltered
and sheltering space turns into the path leading toward the goal which lies
"ahead."

It is the destiny of the people who journey here to be "on the way." They
have given up their home and know that they have been "sent forth." They
know that they have come from somewhere and that they are going somewhere, that they have an origin and a destination, and they know, too, that this
way leads from God to God and that therefore it is a sacred way. They know
the spiritual meaning of the body which has itself already been "given
direction" and shown into the way. To be sure the Lord is no longer "in
their midst" for this train has no "midst"—it has only the goal, far out on

the edge of the world; but he has promised the people that he will "be with them" every day up to the very end. "With them" is also the grace of God, their shining consort. In going their way, this people consummates sacred history and this consummation is their peculiar act of worship. For them, "way" is sacred service.

In this marching army the men stand shoulder to shoulder, each man a link in a chain, each chain a rank. The next ranks stand a step ahead and a step behind, and many weave together into the order of the marching column. At the very front stands the leader. He, too, is facing in the same direction, and like all the others, he, too, is a man on the way.

This form is strict, and if by "love" we mean only what comes into being in the closed ring, then this form is lacking in love. Here no eye looks into another, here no man looks to his fellow—all look ahead. The warm exchange from hand to hand, the surrender from human being to human being, the circuit of heart-felt communion—all are lacking. Here, each human being stands alone within the network of the whole. Shoulder to shoulder in straightened lines they stand, one behind the other, added up into the whole, every man linked to a neighbor at each of the four points of a right-angled cross. The bond which binds each one to the others is cool and precisely measured—actually it is only a bond of the pattern and not a bond of the heart: one man goes ahead of him, another behind him, two go beside him and all go together; he sees into no one's face, two of his neighbors he sees only out of the corner of his eye and one he does not see at all; in space, one is given ahead of him, one behind him, two at his sides. Thus all are woven into the whole in the same way and each one of them is the starting-point of such a cross. In the way-form each one is left alone within the whole, the heart is isolated. The people cannot feel heart-felt warmth for one another since this pattern has no heart at all.

In the ring all this was completely different. There the people were united into the warm and inward form. Their union was based in the common center and in all the individuals who clung to it as "open stars." Thus each person was a little piece of the common ring. Even his own two eyes held intercourse with one another since both were directed to the near center so that together they saw one single image. Neighbor and neighbor were turned a little toward each other as they stood, for between them ran a short stretch of the ring, and the curvature which resulted when they both looked to the common heart turned them just enough toward each other so that they became one.

And yet this most intimate of all forms is not as direct as is often thought. Ultimately, it is only through the many eyes that this form is founded in the common center. It is this center, lying outside of each individual, which turns the neighbor into a brother and the folk into a community. Here, too,

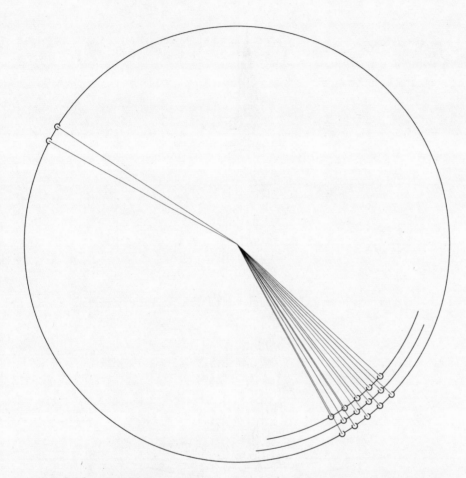

no man looks directly to another—they see each other across the center. And where the people stand ring within ring, only the concentric structure of the ordering connects the man ahead with the man behind: one ring passes into the other through the center.

Yet strict is even this most inward of all the forms of love: the moment the ring opens the power peculiar to it is broken. Now, in the "way-form," the people relinquish forever the old form of their love. Straightening their ranks, they surrender the final remnant of the ring-form which, in the "open ring," still belonged to them. At last they resign themselves, realizing that

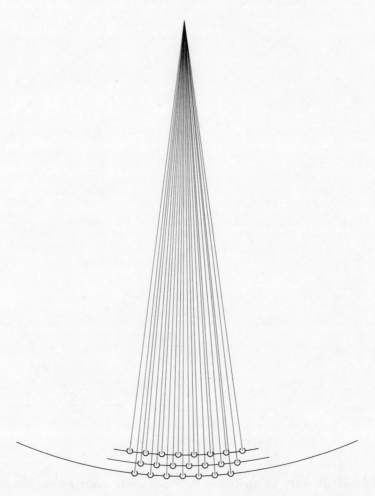

they must go their way without love in that earlier sense, and that they are
meant to remain alone. Then, out of their disappointed hearts, now forever
solitary, the new form takes shape. Little by little it comes into being. The
real break lies between the forms of the closed and the opened ring—the
latter tends steadily into way-form: the rings gape ever wider, their curvature growing ever flatter. Slowly the people cease to face toward each other
and the prospect of winning back the old form dwindles. The center moves
further and further away and finally this point, the very heart, withdraws

into the infinite distance. Then the eye-beams, focussed thus on the infinite, straighten out into parallel lines and, at right angles to them, the rank forms.

Thus the way-form is that form of the community which comes into being when the shared center of love flees into the infinite: like the ring it is an extreme case. Between the two lie the open rings, gaping ever wider— these are the forms of transition.

Just as the ring is a far stricter form than appears at first sight so this form, too, is richer in love than we at first suppose. And that which happens is ultimately much the same in both of them. Love has assumed a new form, but as long as the structure has a heart and clings to this heart with a lively spirit love remains, even when the heart lies outside in the infinite. As long as all eyes cling to the distant light and as long as the light shines into each heart illumining it inwardly, this form, too, remains a form of communion. The light binds the human beings together. To be sure, this is a bond which comes from one human being to the other on a pathway through the in-finite—the infinite which creates and sustains both and which is common to both. Any finite fulfillment is denied here, since the people share only the center there outside and their common situation before the infinite; and therefore this bond lacks all nearness and directness but is nevertheless overflowing with love. What binds the people here is different from that which bound them so blessedly together in the ring. But it is just as strong and just as profound. When they look into the common light this light makes them stretch out their hands to one another and knits them into a holy chain. The love which they believed they would have to relinquish is theirs again as constancy. This little band on the way, these two, three, five people— they know that they must go to the same goal. The same light illumines them all and knits all of them together. They know that in constancy they are profoundly united and their constancy accompanies each one surely and dependably in the other. And so for them the way-form becomes a form of final love, of love in austere restraint—love translated into new form. This love forms and fills the train, knitting it together, linking its order. To left and right the chains extend out into a dark, uncertain space, and, opened, the last hand reaches out into it. But the light holds the people together so that no one loses his way. Constancy, too, is an ultimate human deed and therefore her strict articulation, seemingly so harsh, is actually a genuine form of genuine communion, although of a communion which appears cool and abstract since it has relinquished all finite fulfillment.

The symbols of wayfaring are the chain, the net and the cross.

We have already discussed the chain. The people are strung together to form it, one beside the other. The law of its formation is abstract: a chain comes into existence when similar links are welded one into another. Thus a chain can become ever longer but it cannot actually grow, for to grow means to unfold out of a center, to bring forth a form little by little, to render a rhythm. But here there is no center. The chain can be cut in half and then its length is the same from each end to the point where it was cut. But this point has no meaning for the form and the chain itself is the same here as at every other point. The chain has no measure. To have a measure means, indeed, to be measured from within, and, growing, to fulfill the inner measurement; it means to be capable of growth and articulation, to

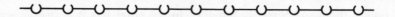

possess an inner limit within which meaningful form comes into being. Of all this the chain knows nothing. A new link can always be added, but this does not change the chain—it is no better, no worse. Endless monotony is the law of its formation.

In the marching column one chain behind the other is woven into the net. This net has the form of a rectangular field which is divided into squares. Human beings occupy the points at which it is knotted.

This form, too, comes into being through simple accretion. Individual is added to individual to form the chain and then multiplied into the field.

In this process the individual experiences nothing. He who entered into the ring was taken up into a higher form which would have been closed to him as an individual. He took part in a creative movement whose outcome was the new communal form. But the individual who happens to find himself in the net takes part in a multiplication of that which he already is. Others are added to him but still this does not result in a higher form. The addition does not change him and does not concern him inwardly; the multiplication, once begun, can be carried on endlessly yet nothing new develops thereby; for the pattern itself the *number* of people who are woven into it is without the least significance, nor is anything changed if some of them are taken away. Neither from the individual nor from the form itself can one know what extent the whole will ultimately assume; that is a purely quantitative question: the net increases in size as long as its source of supply lasts. The ring on the contrary is measured from the very start by that tiny curve formed by two neighbors, even by the two eyes of a single human being.

Thus this form is abstract; it lacks the powers of organic growth. The generative movement is one of uniform flowing, of slow accumulation, and it needs the people only as the material for such uniformity. Within the whole they have value only as points, the net lays hold of them in accordance with their human type and uses them as interchangeable occupants of particular spots. We know such forms in lower nature. Thus do crystals precipitate out of a saturated solution into a network, for in these lower regions building is still only a simple accretion, the movement of adding. This, then, is the right word: here, instead of organizing themselves, the people crystallize.

This idea is unusual to us—we generally think that life has overcome this lower principle. And yet human beings assume this form not infrequently: even if we are loath to admit it, this is one of the great fundamental forms of our being together. This net, inherent even in the structural plan of the body, its design based on the length of the stride and the width of the shoulders, always appears when people must go a common way—even just to walk means to divide up the earth according to the length of the stride. The net is the crystalline form of the streaming crowd. Its amorphous type can be seen every time a mass of people goes to a "meeting" or comes back from one. At the slightest, for instance musical, provocation, this formless streaming changes in an instant into the crystalline order of march—the amorphous form of the mass inclines to the marching order. This order, however, is distinguished in one important way from the crystalline net: it is directed toward a goal. Each link hangs on this goal, each is "open" to it. The chain and the net are not welded shut within themselves, rather are they linked to the goal; throughout their entire extent they are opened toward the end: "open chains."

The cross is the third element of the form.

The net grows together out of many small crosses, each of which marks a human being's place. Man's bodily structure is polarized: one axis runs vertically upward from below, one horizontally ahead in the direction of the way and the third runs at right-angles to it, in the direction of the shoulders. All three axes stand at right angles to one another.

This polar cross, which is represented in living men, must not be confused with the right-angled cross of analytical geometry which is in reality based on the star-form and which starts out from an imaginary point to apportion space in directions of equal value. Here each direction has its unalterable meaning. And, more important, apart from the sideways direction which radiates out to both sides, the movement, while passing *through* man, does not have its origin in him. He is set down within it: "destiny" has given him direction. He does not divide up the world—various movements cross each other in him and he is placed at the point where they intersect. The world is divided up across him and through him.

The cross-form is spaceless. He who stands within it experiences the world as direction. His space-creating power is consumed in rendering the right-angled cross and so is translated into directed movement. It is in this way that the living world is cleft. What is really experienced of the world is no longer spacious vaulting and unbroken fullness but is instead a narrow path opening ahead, rising step by step out of the darkness, then to be lost again behind; and it is also a certain stretching out toward both sides, a reaching out of the hands into the uncertain. This form of partici- pation in the world is strictly linear. Whatever may lie next to the branches of the system is only dimly sensed. The form is put out in the midst of an uncertain world, a world which it must travel but in which it finds no more than the supporting "medium."

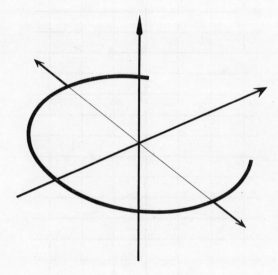

The net, formed by the individual crosses clinging to one another, is also a spaceless, linear structure, since in it, too, there is no spatial full- ness but only directions. World is experienced only as direction and as means in the net. Its inner condition, however, can be compared to that of the "lattice-work" in an iron bridge or in some other "skeletal" structure: the power of the space has drawn together into a network of members and traverses the universe without expanding outward into it. And still this system has a kind of inner space: the tensions stream through the members and are interchanged among them, and in this way the form is made whole. The structure comes into being through simple accretion, yet each addition changes the inner tension in such a way that at each point the whole can be experienced inwardly. Since, in addition, the "lattice" is firmly welded together the various intervals and extensions within it are precisely determined. The individual members are "located" in exact rela-

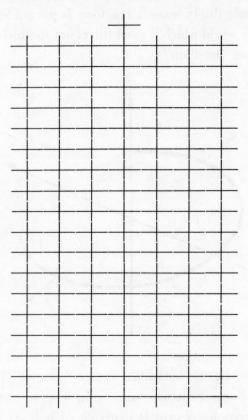

tion to each other and it is this feeling of location which is a metamorphosed feeling of space. This feeling is determined by the strange exactitude of the measurements. We know the feeling of desolation which overcomes us when we go through the streets of a city which is built according to a right-angled plan but which has no center: much room yet no space.

Two people on a common way experience their togetherness not only as accretion but also as exaltation to a form. The little group experiences its quality of three-ness, four-ness, five-ness not only as addition—it experiences its number as a quality, as a particular value. The group perceives that its union has a certain extent, that a certain number of members make up a field of a definite size. A thousand people, even ten thousand, experience the size of their formation. The procession receives an inner measure from its total number; the individual knows that it is of exactly this number that he is a member and this number becomes for him a part of that form under which he experiences his own standing within the whole. He knows his own particular place and he knows that the distances within the field and all the interrelationships arising from them are assured. The ordering is preserved in the midst of flux and it gives the members a relative sense of space and a relative security.

This experience then becomes a part of the supreme fact that the whole structure is journeying through the world. All this can be compared with the experience of a voyage. On board ship everything has its set distance from everything else: everything and everybody has its proper place. A rigid set of orders governs the duties of the seamen and at the same time the whole ship is sailing across a dangerous ocean to a distant goal. The ship has little meaning of its own—its construction as well as the well-defined and rigorous work of the crew purpose in each detail the happy completion of the journey and receive their explanation from it. But at the same time they provide the ship's company with the relative assurance that theirs is a good ship which provides shelter and protection; and as they carry out their duties, the men experience the trustworthiness of officers and crew. They know that this discipline, so painfully kept, is well-meant and that it is a symbol of mutual trust. And therefore they obey it willingly. The people are truly at one only in their common destination but below the great and exalted communion in the distant goal of their journey, a small and genuine comradeship forms amongst them, even if it is relative and only valid for a time.

All this belongs together. Way-form is needy, resigning form; and a people whose destiny is "common way" lives without rest, almost without body, on this earth. But they live in a great and daring way. They have risked their whole existence on the goal. Their space is consumed in representing the way, no form of living growth pervades their wretched assemblage. Yet deep within is consummated the secret process between parting and end, and this gives them the measure of great history; step by step the journey comes to pass. On the outside this form resembles the forms of lowest nature. But the low "chain" is welded shut in itself, one link is tied into the other and none can escape; the natural chain multiplies the wretchedness of the natural ring which is trapped in itself. The "chains" of the way-ordering, however, are woven together out of open rings. Their union has its root in the goal: this we call an "open chain." Nor has this "net" anything to do with the net in which nature is caught. Here the links are not tied into one another nor is one row knitted into the next: instead all are linked to the goal—from one row to the next a step of history is taken. This form is founded in freedom and its bond is constancy. Uniformity pervades it but this uniformity rests in the fact that all are looking ahead.

Those who are settled down in the closed forms will never understand this pilgrimage. They know the way only as means—for them, way leads from one landed property to another. But to journey throughout a lifetime, a whole people, an epoch on the way, way as the anatomy of existence —to them this can only be meaningless and unbearable. Way wholly as the service of God—to them this sounds like blasphemy and the moment they gain an understanding of the form as such it will seem still worse, like some frightful derangement of the abstract mind, like a monstrous temptation. If way-form is so—so spaceless, so monotonous, so cold— then it cannot become sacral, since anything which, by its very nature, is incapable of harboring a hallowed meaning is incapable of becoming a sacred vessel.

One truth remains among such reproaches: this people has a hard lot. They have no home. The form makes them fugitive on the earth, it consumes them in representing an endless process of consummation. The earth is but the material which bears their train, it is not a staked claim. This folk founds no cities, cultivates no countryside. The things which other peoples take so for granted—that man, sheltered in God, also has a home in the world, that wherever there is sacred form, a reverent delimitation occurs, and that the building of a church means primarily the enclosing of a piece of the world which has now become as God originally intended it to be—all these ideas are foreign to this people. The goal is eternal and sacred, the form reaches out to it as the form of the sacred means to the sacred end. But even simply regarding it as "form" (which indeed it is, in a pre-eminent sense) would be a defection, this would divert the eye away from the goal and the form would instantly disintegrate. And so it is good that this form has no charm: its rigorous austerity is its especial virtue. This people has only the choice between relying utterly and completely on God and so of becoming wonderfully great, or of losing, with God, the last chance of an existence worthy of men. These people must risk themselves utterly on their eternal goal—even in the simplest things they have none but the final choice. Whatever might remain after their defection would be wretched and this their wretchedness could not be hidden. Their debasement soon becomes evident whereas other peoples, long after their defection, are still able to parade in the hard shell of a spherical form which the Lord has long since emptied of meaning.

This form does not suffice in itself. It is bearable only as an exalted chainwork in the light, risked toward the eternal goal. If it defects from this, it plunges into the lower realms. Yet the closed form does not suffice either. The moment it actually closes, it, too, becomes a form of despair. This fate would be common to both. Before God, neither form is superior to the other. The one is bolder, the other more beautiful, but each in its own way is fit for the highest.

Apparently the truly pioneering organ is not the foot but the eye. By itself the foot goes astray and in the darkness its steps soon return again whence they started. But the eye sees the sun and the stars, these give it direction and the eye sets the foot aright. Thus it was the *light* which created

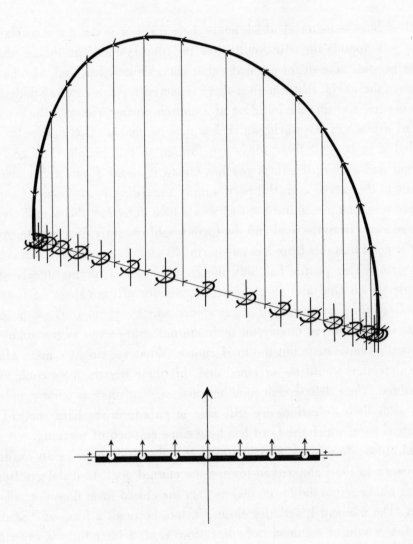

the road the people travel. Their way became, as it were, a second light-way, a new form of the light's path. The peoples follow in the wake of the sun and the pathway of their history leads across the earth as that straight line which connects the point where the sun rises with the point where it sets—their way is the precipitation of the great path on which the sun journeys across the heavens.

Actually it is the light which is the polarizing power. And hence in the cross given in the human body, the axis which signifies "way" may be likened to a magnetic unit which is polarized toward the light (and consequently in the opposite direction toward the darkness). When all these polarized elements are fused to one another to form the grate, an im-

mense magnet results; and within it each little rod fastens to the next in such a way that a positive pole always lies next to a negative one. Figuratively, this structure may be represented as a striped field in which light and dark stripes alternate and which itself begins in darkness and ends in light. Moreover each element is made up of a dark stripe and a light stripe.

Here we may mention that the vertical axis of the polarized-cross which passes through each human being bears a certain relation to the sun, since this axis is directed toward the zenith. There the sun stands at its highest point. And this experience merges with that of the overcoming of gravity, although astronomically the sun's position at the meridian has nothing to do with the center of the earth. Here it is again evident that the real world in which men live and die and effect their salvation, the world, too, of all the great thinkers and givers of form, the world of the poets and the builders, has little to do with the constructions of mathematicians and astronomers. In this world the night is deep and the day high and there is great meaning in the fact that the movement of life seeks the sun's meridian and that despite this the eye rests on the rim of the horizon and not on the zenith; and there is meaning, too, in the fact that the path of the sun crosses the horizon only twice, once in the early morning and once in the late evening, so that the sun comes down to the earth at the very beginning and again at the very end. Men have always believed that the great pathway of their life, to which each of the many daily steps makes its contribution, leads from God to God and is therefore "sacred way." But where way turns into divine service, its direction reverses. The pathway of prayers runs from sunset to sunrise. Praying, the people turn back to the east. They abandon the historical way; they interrupt its natural process and, in a majestic reversal of the sun's path, they revoke the natural course of the world and turn to face the mysterious spot where the light first rises. The people move into the source of the sun. They make all the courses of history flow back toward God. And thus their train itself becomes prayer and sacrificial procession.

This whole ordering cleaves to the eternal light, each individual is open to it and it is the light which links the open rows together. If we look closely we see that each of these "open chains" is an extreme case of the open ring, for each one is a tiny piece of a ring of infinite radius. If this ordering were to be carried out completely its members would come together. And thus it becomes evident that this ordering is a tiny piece cut out of the endless perimeter of an infinite circle. This means that the ordering is a segment of an infinite star-image about the sacred light in the center. In the same way each row clings to the light and thus the entire train is a segment of an infinitely concentric world ordering. Between row and row lies infinity. Each row clings directly to the light, and in standing one behind the other they lay down, step by step, the progress of a history which is effected toward eternity or which grows out of it. The whole ordering is a segment of the eternal star and its ranks are the precipitation of an eternal history. The people which gathers to form this ordering enters into the ground-plan of eternity. They confess themselves to be a tiny piece of the endless star-image surrounding the eternal light and they make themselves into the material of this light's sacred history.

But this history is of infinite extent and the individual steps are so small in comparison with it that all differentiation disappears and uniformity pervades the structure. The people who make themselves a part of the eternal star-image relinquish all hope of reaching their fulfillment in a finite form. They dare the whole. This sacred uniformity, however, has nothing to do with that uniformity which man shares with the lower things: with the uniformity of the repeatable, of the species as a means to an end, with that uniformity whose symbols are the numbers which slaves bear or the shackles which chain them to one another; with the mechanical rhythm of masses degraded to political tools or of bodies and souls debased to the level of matter. The sacred uniformity intends something completely different. In an utterly exalted and absolute sense it intends man as such, as he stands before God. Constituted in way-form, the people renounce all transient ties and unite in the final things which are common to all of them. It is to the *species* that they bear witness, yet not to the species as the carrier of lower functions, as the principle of subhuman drives and arithmetical increase—but rather to the species as humankind, as the thought of the sixth day of creation, as that which God intended when, after creating the stars and the plants and the animals, he created man. When all these individuals, without giving up what more they might like to be or to have for themselves, move into a common ordering in which all of them together express nothing more than that they are human beings before the creator, and when they thus constitute themselves in the ultimate thing which they have in common, in their humanity, then this is honorable and great. And it is also hard.

In the ring, human history united itself before God and besought him to bless its bond. Here men enter in before God who are bound to one another only in their creaturehood, who have nothing ultimate in common before him but their bare humanity. That species enters in before the Lord which shares a common destiny before God, they declare their solidarity within it man by man, drop by drop in the stream of human history, grains of sand upon the shore of the human race. In this great monotony the individual forgets to plead his own particularity. He transposes his own meaning into the creator. It is as a participant in a thought of the creator, who intended all men, that his being added into spiritual uniformity becomes possible. Each one of these tiny elements is polarized toward God in the same way as is the whole form, each tiny drop streams toward him in the same way as does the great stream of mankind. Man's highest destiny is his being summoned, his being on the way, and inasfar as this recurs in the individual, he shares in a legitimate manner in a true monotony of the theological situation. In this great order of march the people are united only by the common law of their final destiny.

A people on the way has no altar. Had they the altar, that sacred spot where God enters the world, the way would be at an end. They would have a holy possession and in it they would find rest. As long as they continue on their way, God is remote from them, he is outside, going there ahead of them and they direct their procession toward him.

For this people, God is the especial danger and not the world. They have renounced the world and they leave it to move toward the mysterious origin of the light. They pursue the light relentlessly. Their entire life has become for them a journeying; their poetry dreams of the hidden cathedral which can be found only by the utterly pure and even their wars are crusades to a sacred place. Their entire being and their entire power are consumed in sacred journey. And yet they cannot come to God's dwelling, for the horizon flees ever before them. They would like to come into what lies beyond their history yet this beyond withdraws. The people move endlessly toward their goal, yet the goal goes ahead of them and the way stretches out across desolate earth. The great reversal of all worldly history marches on: in the people God grows in secret, within them his grace increases; but they seek him out ahead and come no nearer to him.

And so they suffer their terrible disillusionment. They realize that God will never be reached as long as they go toward him, that although this sacred way corresponds with the direction to God yet that this direction never ends and that man never achieves his goal, not even in the infinite. When the people realize that they have set out upon a way which is devoid of hope, the decisive moment comes.

It may happen that the people despair, thinking that they have been deceived. The light in the distance was the reflection of some earthly gleaming, perhaps of their own small brightness, and they have pursued it meaninglessly. Or, still aware that they have followed an eternal light, yet embittered and desolate, empty and utterly exhausted, they may cease to follow after that which is naught but a mockery to men.

In the moment of despair, ruin grips the ordering. It relapses into itself. The open rings shrink together to form the links of a chain, the people hang without hope in the net of nature. Torn from the sustaining meaning, the individual sinks into the uniformity of the species, of function, of the mechanical pattern. He is ensnared in the desolate forms of chain, grating and net. Abandoned and rudderless, the structure is adrift in the dark world. Where the meaningful path between parting and arrival vanished beneath the surface, aimless drivenness begins, endless journeying into nothing. That thinking is profoundly degenerate whose meaning must be replaced by the mere enactment of an empty movement—this thinking does not support us, nor does it sustain us. Yet this is exactly what men must bear: to persevere in the miserable ordering of the crew and to accept their lot within it. For this does remain. No longer explained and illumined by the fullness emanating from the goal, the context is left over like a ghost—it alone can be relied upon. Thus the order degenerates into its own caricature. The infinite goal was its whole foundation—all its parts were preliminary to this and only in the goal was it sufficient. Left to its own resources, it becomes a mockery, a vain and empty voyaging.

And yet it may also happen that the people remain true to their calling even when their train, utterly spent, disintegrates. Now utterly without hope, they surrender even this, their sacred way, and commend themselves to the Lord without reserve. They are at an end, they can go on no longer and they acknowledge their helplessness. In this very instant the journey is over and God is at hand. Then, suddenly, it becomes evident that the Lord had already planned this outcome when he called the creature on its way, that he designed the whole way to lead to this very end and that from the very first this end was infused into the way to guide it. The last step was contained in the very first and each subsequent one drove the people on toward the end. And when the creature finally gives up reaching this goal—in the ultimate surrender even of this, his eternal hope and his sacred chance—the goal has already been reached and God gives of himself abundantly. Here is altar.

Two spots are now marked on the earth: that of the first turning back, the doorway, and that of the final surrender, the altar. Between them stretches the sacred way and it is clear that it was God who gave it its measure.

God counted and reckoned all these steps ahead of time. That which seemed to be an immeasurable movement which could be continued endlessly was in reality measured and limited and this measure exhausted itself step by step, just as a vessel empties drop by drop to its dregs. The "immeasurable" movement is pervaded by an eternal measure. Beginning, extension and goal together make up an articulated form which consists of two spots—as it were, source and mouth—and of a river which flows from one to the other. The linear progress of sheer increase is embedded in the flow of a form whose bounds are set in eternity. Each drop which falls from the vessel of earth is restored through grace.

At last a house can be planned for the procession and its sacred progress, now that it has found the bond which binds it to the earth.

This house is erected over the "sacred way" and is itself a sacred road. This road begins with the portal. The portal is the place where the people interrupt the course of their history and turn it to face the origin, the place of the first sacrifice which occurred in the very early morning. The great gateway is dark. The road ends with the altar, and the altar stands on broad steps which are like the foremost ranks in the order of march. The altar is the place where the people cease their sacred wandering and hence it is the place of the final sacrifice. It lies in purest, clearest light. Behind it the building is at an end, the building's movement has produced the goal. The people stand between end and end and their standing consummates way.

The further working out of the plan is difficult. In the earlier plans the inner space of the people's ordering corresponded to the structure of the universe. When we rendered this inner space, through the use of the walls and the space of the building, we gave the world her form at the same time—from the inside to the outside the structure was one harmonious composition of people and world intermingling.

Here it is not so simple. The way-form has no real, continuing space. Its net-like structure interlaces a world which is travelled and yet not experienced, which completely loses itself in the uncertain. The inner "locating" in the way-form provides only a "relative space"—what would correspond to it would be an unspanned skeletal structure. The best solution would actually be to give the relative inner space its relative shelter in just such an all-embracing grating. The Gothic church accomplishes this. It engirdles the sacred way with the fencework of piers which then intertwine to form the network of the vaulting. The surrounding space breaks in through this trellis-work and is dark in its lower part and light up above. This is the precise

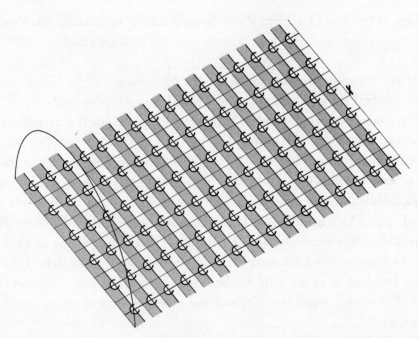

expression of what occurs in the way-form. It is insurpassable. The comparative space of the network is transparent to the space of the universe and the design works the two together contrapuntally.

Another possible solution of the task would be to put the procession into a very deep defile: an arching tunnel, at once wall and roof, would stretch from portal to altar. One end-wall is dark, the other light. Here, too, there is only a relative space, for this vault is in constant movement lengthwise: each of its cross-sections is at work on the sacred way. It encircles the central axis, which is at the same time the axis of the procession, and drives it onward. The encircling movement creates a center path and this in turn creates the vaulting. This vaulting provides as much shelter as one finds under an open archway and possesses as much space as one finds there: space in incessant transition. At the same time the vaulting represents the world through which the procession is journeying, since, for the train, this world is path and gateway, too.

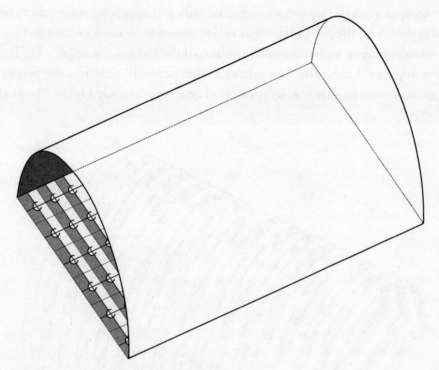

What should be behind the altar?

There is no "behind." With the end of the way, the building, too, is exhausted, the final step has been taken and the light is at hand. The procession is like a magnet, ending as suddenly as it began. Darkness was in the first cross-section, light is in the last, beginning and end are suddenly present. It would be wrong to put a device at the end corresponding to the apse which, in the second plan, opened up an eternal vista. The light is *here*, there is no longer a beyond. The light was ever the hidden accompaniment of the journey and at the end this truth "comes to light." The light was lucent help for every step. It reaches back to the very door, its history reaches back to the very first beginnings. It was the light which polarized the very first link and forced the very first step; its "dwelling place" extends over the entire train. But this separation—which, indeed, the word "with" also expresses—subsides only in the very end: the people unite with the light.

An apse would be legitimate and valid only if it sought no more than to be an enclosure of the end point—that is if it sought to be not a radiant star but a concave mirror, gathering into the altar all the light of the entire way. The next step would naturally be a mirror as the rear wall, reflecting the procession back into the darkness in opposite order—this already hints at the next plan.

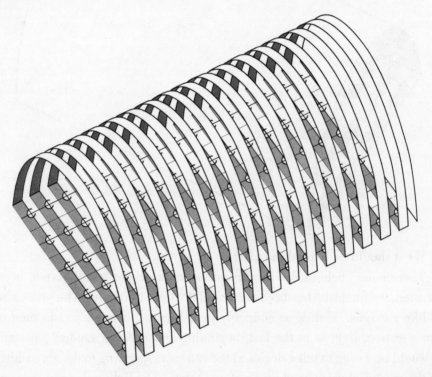

Therefore the span between beginning and end is neither completely dark nor completely light. Its own proper coloring is that gray which is a mixture of the two. This gray does not result from a light at the end being reflected on the neutral vaulting but is rather the very color of the span itself. This world lies in twilight.

But we can also make its mixture apparent by dividing the vaulting into rings, alternating wall and window and hence darkness and light. Then each

step receives its own portal and beyond each one lies a little bit of light.
Usually this is rendered in such a way that the procession is accompanied by
a chain of windows high in the wall which in turn are separated from one another by transverse arches (the relation below-above also plays its role here).

No other structural concept has so glorious a history as the "sacred way."
In this connection we usually think of the medieval processional churches
which unfold this idea in such magnificence. Rows of pillars and great arches
bound and exalt the relative space of the holy pilgrimage. Remote and incalculable, the surrounding space flows round about it, forcing its way in at
the arcades. A darkness rich in mystery rules without. The way is laid from
west to east: the space climbs steeply and from above light falls upon the
path—a rectangular space barely hinted at, an open clearing in God, far
down on the chasm floor sacred path through sacred darkness, high overhead
sheltered by the shining vault, light its consort. No more than the space of a
road, a narrow path through uncertain world, yet of great solemnity and
noble proportion.

But the history of this idea goes back much further.

The early Christian basilica, too, is way, with its solemn procession of
gate-house, courtyard, vestibule, nave and apse.

The frieze of the Parthenon shows way, a people in solemn, sacred procession.

But above all the temples of Egypt are way. The people who lived by the
great river experienced their life as a stream and they built their temples as
sacred rivers bearing the pilgrim now through the monotony of endless rows
of pictures, now through gateways guarded by high towers, through spacious
quiet courtyards, then once more through broad hallways, through great,
dark rooms into which, from above, a meagre light fell which accompanied
the way, then through smaller rooms. The path grows narrower, the group
which is permitted to travel it grows smaller and smaller and finally the way
ends in a tiny chamber. Within it stands the sacred barque—not a shrine but
still another ship. The later the period, the more tedious the way. The suc-

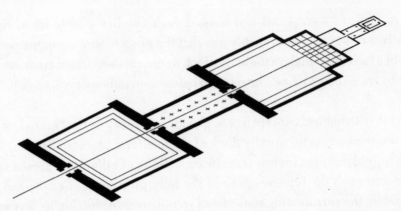

cession of rooms was repeated over and over: portals, courtyards and halls were placed in front of the early core. The chains of rooms accompanying the way of the soul through the phases of the next world were also designed in this late period. They continued endlessly, for it turned out that new phases had always to be added. The idea of the way became a great affliction for this people, they found no end. And this ordeal was real since the esoteric way is in fact without end and utterly without hope. But this people could not acknowledge this to be true and so these temples were documents of despair.

Although these buildings still grip us directly and profoundly today, it is nevertheless difficult to say what was really intended in them. A way, of course, along the central axis—that is easy to perceive—and a way which must really be travelled and which was not intended simply as an image or a perspective. But what does all this mean?

When we walk through these buildings—and they were intended to be walked through—their form unfolds for us into time: out of contiguity grows continuity. We experience the buildings as a sequence in time and this sequence is beset with the most varied experiences. In the gateway the pilgrim experiences end, faltering, darkness, the uncertainty of transition and then the joy of coming out into the new space which opens wide before him. There are parts of the buildings which are clearly meant to be quiet resting places—here the people should spread out, these great rooms are like great ponds with inlet and outlet. Little by little the pilgrim comes into the center where he experiences the space centrally; as he goes on he leaves this room behind, a new passage lies ahead of him and perhaps beyond it a part of the building awaits him which is itself nothing but progress and transition, its central axis marked off by monotonous rows of columns, windows and beams which advance in strict, unvarying procession.

He experiences the structure as spatial sequence. The sequence consists of room, gateway and again room. And so for him the form of the building cuts its steps into time, it becomes a slow progress interspersed with sudden transitions—it becomes something that happens: and little by little he understands that here a sacred history is written down.

These buildings are images of historical time. In them life renders itself as history: it is a continuous course. But this flow is not simply constant, it is built up out of closed "spaces of time" which touch each other. At the point of contact life, transformed into a new phase, moves on. The spaces of time have various forms. Some are of great spaciousness, so broad and still that the way leading through them almost loses itself. Others rooms show the way-form clearly, they advance step by step until their measure is fulfilled and the old phase bursts out into the new. Room and portal attest to two different forms of historical time: a gradual increase prepares the precipitate change.

This wise image of history is not as simple as those modern constructions whose historical time swings like a sine curve about an imaginary axis, eternally repeating the same phases. Nor is it as simple as the ideas of an unswerving ascent nor as the opinion that history is the inexhaustible source of surprises. Hence it is truer. This image knows of repetition; for it, time, as history brings it forth, is the time of clocks: the heart of history beats in an eternal rhythm and it is into this rhythm that history dates itself. But this time contains the secret measure which fulfills itself, the hidden ripening. The "space of time" is filled with repetition, form gives it measure and abrupt transition ends it. Not the wave alone, but the waves of the river, its source and its mouth, everything together, are the form of history. Or the form may be likened to the drop which slowly gathers until it is heavy enough to free itself, whereupon the new influx causes a new drop to form and so on, until the vessel is empty. Or to the earth itself which deposits a geological stratum in an accrual lasting thousands of years, then marks it off with a line no thicker than a hair and then precipitates another stratum on top of it.

Thus that which is built here along a way as a succession of buildings is intended to be the form of historical time: history is experienced as a way, as a flowing, and at the same time as an architectural condition. The holy rhythm of a purifying process is borrowed from life and is then recorded as architectural form. And in walking through it we may read this form backward into time.

The roots of the process are not very clear. Apparently they involve a mysterious "storing up" of the courses and the stuffs of history, yet it is not easy to see how this is possible.

Seemingly the primary asumption is that historical time can appear in two very different ways, as process and as condition, and that at any time its process can be removed and stilled to condition. The events can climb up out of their own stream. Transformed into great statues, they stand on the shores of the river in which they are mirrored. They are like quiet swimmers, motionless on the bank, staring into the stream and waiting for the moment to spring into it once more.

History can be stored up, and this is not something exalted, it is not a kind of "immortalization" as people used to think, but rather one of the simplest and commonest qualities of all occurrences. It happens every day: an object leaves its visible surface behind on the photographic plate in all the fortuitousness of the concrete moment, or it leaves its sound on the groove of a phonograph record; a speech is taken down; the table at which I sit, the study, the house, the city, each preserves the moment in which it was "erected." And this happens completely incidentally and without much reference to whether this moment was a mean or a great one. The things which are stored up are certainly not "eternal" at all, rather are they slumbering happenings, or bits and pieces of them, perhaps just non-essentials which happen to be left over. They are congealed as they stood and as they happened. They still live completely in their last moment and in it they are "contemporary," even when this moment itself may have been over for a long time. Fairy tales tell how a spell freezes the world in the midst of an ordinary day, every movement is preserved as a half-finished gesture to be completed only thousands of years later when the spell is broken. This spell occurs constantly around us. Stored-up history exists in the present like a sleeper in time, indeed, in two times: inwardly it lives wholly and completely in the old moment which was the last it experienced, outwardly it is completely present as an "object," as "material." These remains can be worked with, thrown away, broken up—they are a material very much within reach. With their help the old condition of which they are the remains can be reconstructed scientifically. They can also be awakened. We can take hold of the events themselves by means of their locked and left-over remnants and can force them to transform themselves back into life. For the musician the old score is music once more, for the poet the old page again poetry.

This is all very difficult to explain. We might think, and it has been thought, that no event passes away and that all of them are still present. The event happens as it were doubly. It occurs once as the moment which passes and here it is inwardly linked with what went before it and with what follows it: it comes out of the former and merges into the latter and leaves nothing behind. It remains in the present and exists only in the present—the past passes away for its stuff is consumed into the new moment. But at the same time everything happens forever, too. It is irrevocable in just the way that it happens and by the very fact *that* it happens. And with all its accidental qualities it remains recorded in the book of history. There is a place where it is stored away. This is not a mythical place, not some spot in the legendary depths—myth and legend are indeed the present's poetic answer to this palpable presence of the past which is so frightening to men—but rather the place of the second history, the place where the things are preserved untransformed. It is as if all the things which are no longer meant to appear on the barren stage of life were put away into a gigantic store-house and as if the remains which still stand about the scene are the very incomplete catalogue of this collection. They lie close together, life plays now a little with this one, now with that, leaving the others quietly to gather dust. But they would not be here if history were not built on storing up—and also, if they were not here life would have no plaything.

The ancient architects apparently understood how to use these qualities of the historical process with great intelligence. They deposited history in buildings, the revolutionary event which "entered" abruptly became portal, the flowing course space.

He who followed the sacred way awakened the age-old history and entered upon its exalted course. And yet the means of the ancients were quite limited. The only thing they could do was to lead their initiates along the endless rows of figures beside the way, letting them read what they found there. These buildings are like holy books whose words can be traced by finger and eye. He who wishes to experience them must go the laborious way on his own feet.

Something else came to their aid, and this was the most important thing: the fact that history can be purified, clarified and celebrated, and that then, without losing its concreteness, it becomes universally valid. Life can be heightened to its most exalted form and is then valid for all. History becomes the great commandment into which the individual yields his life in order to exalt it to its own true and worthy form. The early architects interpreted life with great care, they exalted and expanded it into the great and the important, they worked out its majestic contours and then they stored up and preserved the coherent oneness of this lofty life. The "natural" condition of history is comparable to a store-house and the natural landscape to a rubbish heap full of significant remains. But here history became a careful collection and its catalogue became the recorded melody of an exalted process. The staticness of time was used to make the eternal teachable and real. These buildings are sacred teachings of the hierarchical structure of life. They are founded in the idea that the course of the sacred way is exemplary historical sequence. When we go this way the sacred succession of time is taken out of its state of preservation and lived again, its age-old scroll is proclaimed anew.

Not long ago, Desiderius Lenz, who founded the school of painting at Beuron and who also outlived it, once more attempted to bring to life the idea of the "sacred way." His concern was the re-establishment of a church architecture growing out of the sacred theme and he devoted a great part of his life to the "design of a liturgical church," without, however, meeting with success or understanding. With these attempts he stands alone in his century, which was in love with forms and which shrank from content—and he stands almost alone in ours, too.

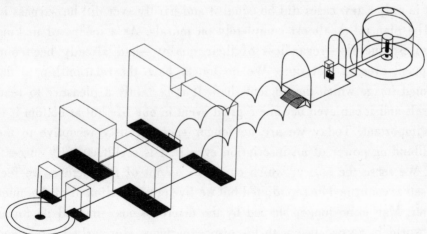

Lenz built up his plan as a single great process.

The succession of spaces corresponds to the succession of periods within the history of salvation. When we walk through the building we read on

the walls the sacred history of the world from its origin to its glory. The
quiet life of history within the liturgical rite is developed architecturally
out of its inner periodicity. Here the architect is clearly convinced that the
flow of the history of salvation is universally valid, that it even reveals
the primal rhythm of grace, and that when we repeat this flow we experience grace as history—an exalted thought.

As we have said, what Lenz actually sought was overlooked in the
criticism of his somewhat inadequate form. He did not have at his disposal
the architectural speech which we possess and he had to make out as best
he could. At bottom he returned to the mathematical forms even if he
found them in archaic styles. But consider what the other churches and
secular buildings looked like in his time!

Aside from this, we can at first hardly understand how this man on his
lonely way could penetrate so deeply into the foundations of genuine religious building. But at closer inspection it becomes more understandable. He was a disciple of the Egyptians, he unlocked the profundity of
the Egyptian theme and attempted to expound it in a Christian manner.
Yet in only a few cases did he equal it and hardly ever did he surpass it.

The plan relies almost completely on murals. As a means of making
manifest, murals—regardless of their quality—had already been out-
stripped, even at that time. We no longer have the relationship to the
painted image which the ancients had. It is certainly a pleasure to read
murals and it can even become a great event in our life but at bottom it is
not important. Today we are no longer spontaneously receptive to the
spellbinding power of an inscription even if it is architecturally successful. We sense the answer which comes to us out of the picture, we feel
ourselves confirmed or repudiated but we live our own life out of the inner
center. Man is no longer shaped by the macrocosmos—instead he forms
the world in accordance with his own experience: formerly he received
his measure from the building, today he gives his measure to the building.
The arts have learned to serve life (this is the only legitimate way to speak
of functionalism or of a humane basis for our architecture,) and now the

structure of the building proceeds out of the inner ordering of the people for since the times of the Egyptians the sacred happening has moved out of monuments and into men.

Thus Lenz would have had to put the sacred history into men as an inner flow, and out of this he would then have had to derive the structure, just as we seek to do. His structure is *processio*. This however presupposes that the divine service itself consists in a slow advance; simple proceeding would have to be cult and the liturgical progress of the people and of the building would have to run parallel.

But this is not at all the case with Lenz. The entire architectural process is idling, since, at bottom, despite all his historical mysticism, Lenz used the building only as a housing for the liturgy, with the people standing in front of the altar. To be sure he developed beautiful ideas for the liturgical part of his design, too; the church should, as he says, have a "throbbing heart," the empty table of sacrifice; and its "head" should be in "repose," the round secluded space of the sacred presence—this differentiation is fruitful. But the murals and the structure of the building have no connection at all with the liturgical part of the design—the liturgical process develops out of the altar and the spatial procession has nothing to do with it.

The author can hardly have realized that here he had reached the vital question and that upon the answer given it depends the Christian succeeding of the way-form.

In its natural dynamism, the way-form is endless. For it, God's dwelling lies on the horizon in the vanishing point. Or the sacred way is given to this form as unrest, as sacred direction. Or, lastly, God may be simply "ahead" of it: he goes ahead of the steps and yet not one of them attains him—it seems as though each next step must overtake him, yet he too advances one step further. But in no case does this way come to an end of itself unless it happens to be cut off prematurely. A people on the way may possess relics and symbols and pledges of the divine constancy which they carry with them on the journey, but they have no landed property, their ordering knows of no altar.

It is just at this point that the new, the Christian element enters: an end is given the infinite road because it came to an end in Christ. From the way-form alone we could not know that the altar stands at the front: we can know this only from the history of salvation where the end has already happened. The people are fused into a history which has still to be lived but which has already come to an end— to an end in which it found salvation and conquered death. Fused into this history, the people take part in the final victory and yet at the same time they must still travel the way. This is the decisive reason why "sacred way" can be Christian form. Every design of a "processional church" which sends the people on their way and brings this way to an end in the altar must rest upon it.

Lenz also lacked another necessary but most modern concept: that of standing form as inner process. He had at his disposal only the old means and the present task is very difficult to solve with them alone.

If we wish to celebrate the sacred process as an actual moving forward, then the altar must be built as a sanctuary to which the people fight their way through many difficulties. The Christian way-form must be polarized: here the people on their way and there the sacred dwelling place of the end which has already happened. But with this the difficulty arises that the blessed end which constantly acompanies the procession should finally "grow out of" it since God is "with" his people. And there is the second difficulty that the people themselves and the grace accompanying them are the building material of which this end is made.

The medieval processional churches and the churches of the East partially succeeded in overcoming this difficulty. The sacrament from a previous service is "stored away," the spot where this sacred storing away took place becomes the goal of the next pilgrimage, and in an actual advance the people finally unite with it. One consequence of this idea is that a small, consecrated group administers the service at the altar in a space which is separated from the people—for indeed at the beginning they are still "remote"—and that finally the people may draw near to this area. Representatives are sent out from the people into the space where the end has already happened, that there, like a lowest order of angels, they may celebrate a heavenly liturgy. All this provides a completely correct and wonderfully beautiful representation of the Christian way-form; perhaps its only shortcoming is that it presupposes an all-too-strong feeling for genuine representation, hence risking a polarization which almost verges on cleavage, and also that its design is very difficult.

All the other accusations made today against the medieval solution are groundless but they do show that our own time is hardly capable of consummating it as living form. Nor do we need this any longer for since medieval times we have gained the idea of form itself as consummation. Today we know that, simply in the concentrated existence of a form, a real process can run its course without the form having to stir outwardly. In a ring the circling movement which created it goes on uninterruptedly, in a building the process which constructed it is being carried out continually: in the heaviness of block on block gravity is constantly conquered, the arch is a constant casting. Thus a form can be designed in which the movement of the way is continually running its course from beginning to end but which nevertheless "stands" as a whole, just as a river "stands" between its source and the sea or a discharge between anode and cathode. Within the figure time is an inner flow and life trickles incessantly through the quiet form. Seen in this light, it is not necessary to lead the individual along an endless way, he can also be placed in the midst of the form's flow. He need not be sent along ever more lonely roads, he can also be set within the whole in such a way that he is alone beyond all telling.

As they "stand" in their way-ordering, the people accomplish the way inwardly. In a succession of phases the quiet form consummates inwardly that history which we have been describing.

At first there is the phase of "early parting": a young people moves toward its creator. The holy light stands in the east as their guide, and trustworthy, too, is the consort of grace. Thus, on a dreamlike path, rides the king in Bamberg, his body unknowing, certain of the goal and blindly certain of the way. His people are linked in the measure of their small and calculable number. He leads them through broad archways and already they face the reflection of eternity. The light high above accompanies each step of their way and in falling illumines a pathway through the midst of the half-dark space.

Then there is the "solemn holy procession" beneath the midday sun. The people move ahead, their going a solemn celebration. They feel so certain in the light that it hardly occurs to them that they are on the way. The altar is a remote crease in the surface of the earth.

Only when the light begins to die away ahead of them, only when the procession, now inwardly directed into the darkness, begins to despair of ever attaining the end, only then does the dwelling place of the altar slowly rise up: the final obstruction beyond which the procession cannot pass.

Then there is the phase of coming to a standstill and of final surrender and in this moment the altar is the place of sacrifice. And then there is the final phase in which the altar is the dwelling place of the light which is now at hand.

Externally, little changes in the building in all this time but the content and meaning of the various parts are transformed as the phases run their course.

Those churches which are built over one of the early phases of the process, and which are thus primarily exodus or solemn procession or way to evening prayer, are truly pure way-form. The whole people is on the way and hence the priest should look forward just as all the people do. But the two final phases make it permissible for the priest to face the people. We may conceive of this medievally, and then he is their representative who is already standing in the end; but it can also be understood to mean that here God's dwelling no longer lies ahead and that the priest turns the people's prayer back into the second sacred dwelling. He invokes God, God who is "with" the people, and he sends their prayer back into the dwelling place which is given in this "with."

And so, to return to Lenz' plan, really new was only that he exalted the

imitation of the Lord's life to architectural greatness and that he was able
to recognize in the history of salvation the "type" of all sacred process.
This is not absolutely new: the Middle Ages were acquainted with this
idea and we are familiar with it from many instructions in the blessed life,
but for Lenz' time it was a true discovery. Provided, then, that this idea is
correct, that which at first seemed to be simply way-form and which at
closer inspection turned out to be the form of sacred "pro-cess" is, in the
end, the form at the root of the Lord's life. The Lord took on the form
which is at the root of the historical process and represented it in his own
life. Thus he made the course of his own life the measure of all sacred
history. Now there is only one sacred way: the imitation of the Lord in
time and in history. He who seeks salvation must seek it by following the
thread of the history of salvation. Bringing this exalted course anew into
life, he consummates sacred process. And therefore processional churches
are nothing but the imitation of the Lord with the means of architecture.

But even here there is a qualification to be made, a qualification which
even runs against the beautiful early instructions.

Together with the *human* form the Lord assumed the *natural* form
which God gives to history. In history he fulfilled his mission and he
would have completed history in the founding of his kingdom. But at the
same time he assumed the tragedy which is contained in this natural form,
its striving back to the earth and its being contradicted by the movement
which is directed toward God. The natural life which comes from God is
the bearer of the life which moves toward God. This second, inner life of
grace flows toward God, thwarting and disavowing the natural life which
flows away from him. They are fused together yet contrary; with every
step natural life is overcome and at the same time fulfilled. But it is just
this second form which is the substance of the divine service, for it is this
form which continually consummates the sacrificial movement, constantly bending natural life and its history back into the movement of
sacrifice. Hence if our plan is to be a true imitation of Christ—inasfar as

he rendered an uninterrupted divine service—then the one thing it may not do is to reproduce his natural life, his hard road, or perhaps seek to repeat his thwarted kingdom. Rather must it render the other story which is in him, the story which sent him on this way, which frustrated his plans and finally led him into death. Here it is this first history *toward* God which becomes form. The death of the Lord is renewed inasfar as it was destined, the death which came to pass from within, that which lay between his being utterly forsaken and his utter surrender into the Father's open hands. The Lord's death on the cross is repeated in this form, but it is repeated as the dynamism of that grace which, ripening secretly to fullness, increased to death. Here, in individual and community, this inner way is repeated, the dark fate and the secret succour.

If our interpretation of the "sacred way" is correct, then the meaning of this way reaches deep into the eternal. The "sacred way" is the process of eternity. That first secret history hidden in the life of the Lord is the primal history of grace, God's own quintessent movement carried out in unbroken purity. And what happens in everyday life and in its history is a late answer to this first sublime process. The community which goes this way in prayer carries out step by step the ascent of grace itself. In the great doorway they enter the majestic landscape of eternity. Darkness surrounds them like a narrow canyon, and through its midst runs the little pathway of light which is created and led onward by this very darkness itself. The people are taken up into the great movement in which darkness comes into light. Then they are sent back out of the dwelling place of the light, back in the direction of the world and its history.

Thus this plan writes down two histories which fulfill themselves from doorway to altar. Here, in rendering step by step the fundamental form of temporal life, the human beings enter in before the Lord as an historical people. They make the natural course flow backward to the mysterious moment of its creation. As the natural element dwindles, grace increases. And grace forces the way onward.

We may make this setting between death and birth more obvious by grouping the people according to their ages and then placing these groups one behind the other. The procession is then a succession of spaces of time, created out of an inner growth. The present existence of the men implies the earlier existence of boys; and that there is death at the end means that earlier there was birth. Each human being passes gradually through the whole form: he ripens within the union of his group, then to enter into the next. It is disputable whether the children or the old people should stand at the front—in the former case the movement is made to flow backward to birth, in the latter it declines into death. Each yields a good meaning.

The plan is more impressive if we renounce such articulation: the monotony of the way-form then emerges in all its clarity, a people stands reft of all detail, rendered in its most exalted destiny between birth and death and it gives this destiny back to the Creator.

This is also the situation of the masses in the great cities: innumerable people without any intermediate articulation placed before the final things. These masses are threatened in their freedom, the external powers seek to force them into the chain. But they give their answer in the sacred way-form. Is there not something of all this in the churches of our industrial cities where everything is abortive artistically but where, in the almost endless rows of benches, real life has precipitated itself as a marching order?

Sacred Cast
The Dark Chalice

T HE FIFTH PLAN shows the people moving into the new land which has been made ready for them. They are coming out of the distance in a long train. Their journey is almost completed and now they are drawing near to the goal. Opened wide, heaven is waiting. The Lord, sitting at the front, stretches out his arms toward the train of people. (These arms are the angels and the saints high on the walls and also the light which he sends out from the end to meet the procession. The altar is the place where he awaits his own.)

Here a story ends which began when the round space opened to dismiss the people. At that time it was the darkness which opened to face the distant light and here it is the light which opens into the darkness and which receives the train of people coming out of it. At that time it was a putting out to sea, now it is a putting into harbor, and between them lies the way.

The image of the church standing with outspread arms before the Lord, in which we understood the second plan, is answered here by the image of the Lord who receives the people with opened arms. Tired by their way through history, the people are coming to him; and at bottom it is he himself who comes, for he "was with them alway" even to this final blessed day.

Thus this plan is the answer to the second plan. If we wished to represent the entire story, the first opening-up in the second plan would have to be

placed at the beginning, the way would then have to be joined onto it and here the way would come to an end. The figure would then be rendered in its entirety, it would have a dark pole and a light pole; two open forms would face each other, one of darkness and one of light, and the people would be moving into the light one. On the way the two forms would interpenetrate; each segment of the way would have a light part and a dark part, at the far end would be pure darkness and here at this end pure light.

But why should we represent the complete figure at all? Its beginnings have long since sunk into the depths of the past. The people have forgotten their dark origin and now they forget even the toils and troubles of the way. Their hearts are filled to overflowing with the joy of arrival, their eyes look to the light and their feet already tread the sacred ground. This is the only part of the form which is important now. All we need do is to take this part out of the complete figure and to give it form.

This provides us with the basic requirements for the planning.

This structure is simply open roundness. It is not the roundness of the apse, which opens up an eternal vista, then to return once more out of eternity. Rather is it that roundness which is end and shelter, the simple presence of joy, the awaiting light—that into which the people finally surrender themselves as if into an open hand.

The plan consists of the concavity into which the furthermost end of the way discharges. The walls of the way bend into a rounding. Or, one turns around to join the other, thereby describing the curve.

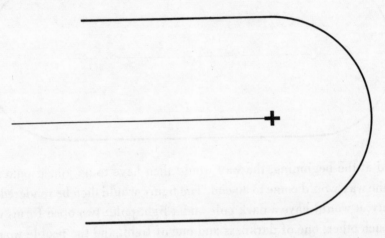

The simplest way of representing this would be to choose a semi-circle as the ground-plan for the rounding, drawing it out at each end in the direction of the tangents. But here a peculiar difficulty would arise. The back wall would form a right angle with the parallel side walls, thus marking off a sort of living space, and this would contradict the meaning of the figure. Therefore we believe it better to choose a parabola for the ground-plan since the parabola is absolutely open—each little section of its course contains openness. If a line is drawn at right angles to the axis, cutting off the curved end, this line, wherever it may be placed, will stand at an oblique angle to the curve; the delimitation of the space remains accidental and does not result from the course of the figure itself. (This is utterly different in the case of the ellipse, whose two chief axes are inherent in its inner course.)

We place the altar in the focal point of the rounding. The walls should be very high and made of a hard, heavy material, perhaps of stone blocks. Or we could execute wall and roof as one single arch; this arch would of course incline upwards toward the front of the building since the ground plan grows wider there.

There should be no windows in the surrounding wall for they would detract from the inwardness of the building: through the windows the sun

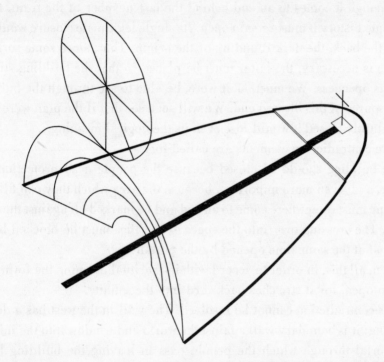

would shine in, whereas the true meaning of this plan is the ultimate presence of light. The rear wall should be lit up by light streaming from the altar and, as in the old apses, Christ could be represented there, his hands and eyes opened wide, full of earnestness against a golden ground. But if there are to be windows, these should be increased along both side walls up toward the crown of the arch overhead.

Somewhere in the western part the space is closed by means of a cross-wall. The space grows darker and darker as this wall approaches. The wall contains the portal and perhaps in its upper part a rose window of deep red. The wall should lie far enough back so that behind the people there is still a great deal of empty space which clearly shows that the procession is at an end.

Here a difficulty arises similar to the one which could not be completely surmounted in the second plan. We may not close this image of homecoming even though it comes to an end behind the last member of the train. Backward into history it must remain open. Its single legitimate closure would be, far at the back, the dark rounding of the origin. Thus, since some sort of a closure is necessary, the latter must be placed so that the building still retains its openness. We must, as it were, be able to see through the building to the source of this blessed end. We will soon see that if the plan were to be prematurely closed it would lose even its theological meaning.

Here contradictory elements are called for:

The building should be closed because the people need protection and shelter, and, even more important, because the area which they can fill with meaning must somewhere come to an end and be marked off against the outer world. The crossing over into the space of sacrifice must be blocked by the wall and at the same time opened by the portal.

Yet in all this, in order to accord with its spiritual meaning the form must remain open, for it stretches backward into the infinite.

This contradiction cannot be resolved. The wall in the west has a double meaning: it is boundary-wall against the world and window into the infinite. The portal through which the people pass in leaving the building has a double meaning: it is exit into the world and gateway into the darkness of eternity.

We must attempt to express this double meaning of the western portion. Perhaps the high surrounding wall, that part of the form which carries the greatest spiritual meaning, could be shaped in such a way as to make us aware that it runs back out of sight, that rearwards it actually has no end. The cross-wall could then be set into it in such a way as to make us recognize that this is a work of necessity and accident This rear wall would have to preserve a certain "transparency" out onto the greater movement into which it is injected. We could make the wall of glass and continue the surrounding wall on beyond it.

Of course this surrounding wall would have to end eventually too, and in addition the meaning of the space would be distorted by the light coming in through the glass. So it would be better simply to make the cross-wall of a lighter, less durable material, thus marking it off clearly from the surrounding wall and revealing it to be a completely different element, an "incident"

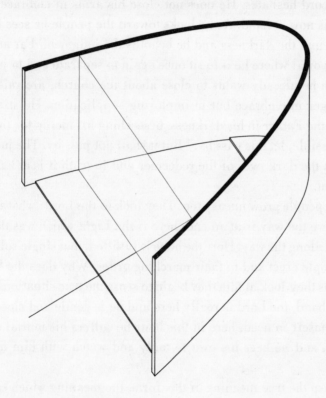

which "happens" here. Beyond that we would have to content ourselves with the oblique intersection of the two walls which fails to produce a right angle. Perhaps the completely different building material and the completely different course of each element of the building would be an adequate expression of what concerns us here, namely that at the point indicated by the cross-wall, man enters the inner space of an eternal movement, but that, seen from the inside of the movement itself, this point of entry is accidental. The law of the cross-wall is only temporal, that of the main figure eternal.

The throng moves into the space.

Now they think that they have come home and the Lord thinks so too. These open arms will close in embrace, heaven and earth will unite.

Yet the Lord hesitates. He does not close his arms in embrace although the church is now at hand. As he looks toward the people he sees back over their heads into the darkness and he beholds the judgment. Far at the back he sees the portal where he is to sit once again to separate and to judge. The arms, which he already wants to close about the church, are raised anew, now no longer in embrace but in imploring supplication. He stretches out his arms to the Father in his darkness, beseeching his mercy for the people: "If it be possible, let this pass by." But it shall not pass by. The judgment is mirrored in the dark eyes of the redeemer and in truth it is at hand in this very moment.

Then the people grow uneasy too. They look to the Lord: what is he waiting for? Here the way is at an end, here *is* the Light which was their guide and goal all along the way. Here the hope is fulfilled, that single solace which held the people erect and in their marching order. Why does the Lord hesitate? Now as they look at him they begin to sense the true situation. The light is really at hand, the Lord is really here and he is gentle and close to them, but he is himself in need, here in this hour he suffers his mortal agony for this people, and he begs his own to tarry and watch with him until all is fulfilled.

They grasp the true meaning of this form, the meaning which emerges so terribly out of the blessed beginning: to be taken up into the open eyes of the Lord, up into his mortal agony; to become one with him and in him to face the darkness which until now had always stood unseen at their back: to look openly with him into the dark end.

This form casts back into history. It sends the people back into the declining branch of the figure, into the fall of a movement which leads at first into the very center of light but which then veers about to fall back into the darkness. The people must remain in their way-ordering. From the altar they are not dismissed into daily life: they are sent into the second part of their sacred journey which leads again to the portal. They must go back along this toilsome way once more, and this time it does not lead into the light. The procession remains formed for the end into which it is sent by the eyes and arms of the Lord. The form remains open to the back and into this openness the people must go forth to their final battle. Thus this form too remains unsatisfied. Just as the second plan did not close because the Lord had gone forth and because his going forth became the bleeding wound of all history, so this plan does not close because the Lord will come once more, and since this second coming lies ahead the end cannot yet come to pass. In the meanwhile the earth remains open and heaven hesitates; and thus the earth can no longer be true to herself nor can she make her way into heaven. Both plans persevere in the frustrated yet honest state of being wounded at the very heart. Only at the very end does the one plan close the other.

A history is enacted in this form. Beginning in joyful anticipation, all parts move into their radiant fulfillment. Yet the fulfillment is deferred. The opened form, which should close as does a fertilized blossom, hesitates. No fruit begins to grow, the form remains opened, indeed it opens ever wider. The end does not come and the people are sent back. A form of deferred closure, of new and ever greater openness into a dark end—that is this plan. What at first seemed to be only an unexpected halt and then grew into a frightful and bitter disappointment, exactly this: the turning back of the movement of homecoming, the renunciation of joy and the quiet submission of obedience—all these things together make up the hard and mysterious meaning of this design.

If we look carefully we see that all this was already foreseen in the previous plan. This plan was "way" and up to the final threshhold it hid what was to occur at its end. Here, this emerges out of its reserve, frightfully becoming form. The moment of transition, of despair and of surrender—the end of the journey and also the readiness of heaven—all this becomes visible. This whole plan is transition, and if we grasp it profoundly it means death— the good death, the dark sacrament which men receive from the Lord's hand.

A church can be built over each point of the rising or the falling way.

Phase by phase, image by image, the structure reveals itself.

The first image is solemn entry.

Splendid, radiant and spacious the roundness waits and solemnly the space draws near to it. High on the walls two rows of shining figures accompany the festal procession. The Lord is entering into his city.

In the second image the church rests with John on the breast of the Lord.

The people have filled the curve and they crowd about the radiant altar to celebrate the supper with the Lord. He is beautiful to them and near, and in the bread and the wine he unites himself with them. But he looks out beyond the congregation and sees the things which are beginning to gather. Yet the people understand little of all this, for to them it is hidden future and they nestle still closer to the Lord. He is near, whereas this other thing cannot as yet be clearly recognized; it is present over their heads, it stands at their back, it entered the room while they, and with them the whole building, were celebrating this final supper on the eve of Good Friday. In the center stands the radiantly shining altar and at the same time this other thing is obscurely at hand. In wall and vaulting it towers high over the gathering, its details lost in darkness. Only the great outline of its form and the general line of its movement can be sensed, in the same way that each of the Lord's sad and loving words on this evening forecasts the coming crisis. Gradually the darkness prevails. Congregation and altar become a last bright speck in the midst of the falling darkness, no breath of wind stirs within the bay into which the first waves of the rising storm are already breaking—final shelter in dying light.

This supper ends when the Lord goes out into the night.

In the third image the Lord goes into the darkness.

A few disciples accompany him a little way, and then, beyond the last three human beings, he takes up the battle once more. He fights for his own life and with it for all that is light and hope in this world. He would like to spare the world the death of the Son of Man and yet he already sees the darkness like an open chalice which he must drink. May the Father not allow it! But the Father, with whose power he has been ever and again victorious up to now, gradually retreats and grows remote. He sends one comfort, one of his angels, and for a moment everything is good. Then it grows dark once more and the comforts which the Father sends are now ever smaller, ever weaker. Then the Lord yields. He awakens the men. What follows is strangely quiet, it seems more to befall the Lord than to be his doing and actually this whole happening is only a late consummation of a first story which happened long ago. At the very end utter forsakeness grips him once more and for the third time he yields himself "into the Father's hands."

Ever since, the Lord's mortal agony has lain on the world. It waxes and wanes but it is forever present. It lies at the heart of all sacred form; wherever there is sacred world the Lord sheds his sweat of blood for its enduring radiance. Some times must suffer through this agony even unto the final submission, some are spared it almost entirely—yet among those whom the Lord took with him into his final agony was John, who understood him more than the others—and sometimes the final victory emerges in promise out of history. But in this temporal world all victories are but ambiguous success, all transfiguration but a passing solace, like the bright chalice which was given the Lord in his direst need.

And so it is certainly right that there are churches which have become forms of the sacred agony, churches in which the final things are summoned into the haunted forms of transition. And yet it is nevertheless the Father who proffers his "dark chalice" there. In the darkness, which, interwoven with the light, was ever an element of our plans, this end is already present, it embraces the closed form in the outermost outline, it went forth with the people and here it breaks in upon them. Here in these "Mounts of Olives of our time" the Lord's dire need, as it lasts unto the very end, has become visible form. Ever higher and ever steeper grow the walls, ever broader grows the empty space. Lost far below in the deep canyon, the little congregation surrounds the altar while round about them and high above them the great happening is accomplished. The flickering light is like the consecrated candle lit beside the dying. It proclaims that the Lord is still with us and that he still suffers his agony.

This is then the final image:

The Lord is dead and they have taken him down from the cross. Mary is sitting there once again, her son, her child who is dead, upon her knees. She looks into his eyes but they are dim and in them she sees naught but emptiness. She embraces his body—in form and shape it is still as she knew it but it is cold and stiff. And so she sits, empty with pain, her countenance mirroring the emptiness of the void. Thus is Mary represented in the late Middle Ages. The Pietàs are at once sacred and terrible, far more terrible than all the images of the torment and torture of the crucifixion. In the crucifixion it is God's Son who suffers, still fighting, still living, still with us. The Pietà on the other hand is silent and this terrible silence says that the Son of God is dead and that nothing but his corpse remains. These images were carved in the late time when the people died of the plague and the body of the church was beginning to decay. Still more terrible images of Mary's lament are the buildings of that time. Every detail of the form is rendered as it was when it was alive, and this with an exactitude as cruel as mockery, but the form is stiff, and evil is already rising out of its desolate emptiness. Here is Mary's second seat, at the outher end of history, in the evening after all is over.

It may be that the Lord has enjoined single periods, even individual men, to mourn with Mary beside his corpse. It may even be that not only his agony and death but also his burial is given in all sacred form, and that although it may emerge more or less sharply, wherever there is sacred form there is also sacred grave. When this most difficult of fates is destined as the particular task of a man or a time, the final consolation may still remain that although the Lord did indeed die and although his body grew pale and empty, the Father in his mercy did not let it fall prey to corruption. The peculiar bitterness of such a calling would lie in the fact that those who answer it may not go forth into the world and to their work but must hold out at the side of Christ's grave by his corpse. They would have to believe that this corpse too is sacred form, and with Mary they would have to go out and buy spices to keep it.

To a time whose task it is "to proclaim the death of the Lord" belongs a church which corresponds to our plan, for the last memory of the Lord shortly before his death must be preserved. But even though this is now only a preserved form, it could be lit up by brilliant light. The altar is stripped, the candles extinguished, and the form of sacred agony still towers about it, left over and become meaningless.

In all these images the same movement is accomplished, if on different levels: the casting movement. Casting is that movement which rises at the beginning, slowly tires under the pull of gravity, curves and falls once more. What consumes the original ascent is gravity, a foreign power, (the inertia of the earth) and yet it is an inner power, too, for the cast object is itself heavy and the heaviness in it wants to return to the earth.

This movement, translated completely into terms of the spirit, concerns us here: an ascent flags under the influence of a foreign and yet inner power and then sinks back into this power once again. And in this process it is a sacred power which causes the ascent and which also consumes it: ascent and fall are movements of the spirit.

This is a dark mystery and will remain so. Still the Lord's words and actions give a certain clue to that which happens here so incomprehensibly. Up to the very last it is light which he represents before the Father, the kingdom of heaven, life eternal, but he feels how it is subject to another law which forces it downward once more. He speaks of this other law as of something which works into the things from an infinite distance. This other power he calls the "will of the Father" and he experiences it as a movement. May it "pass from me," he prays; but if that cannot be, may it then "be done." But when it really is done, when he must die and together with him the whole shining plan of a holy world, then he can only ask why God deserts him—and in this moment he is not so unlike the late Greeks, Niobe and Laocoön, who die with lifted head, on their lips the terrible question, why then the gods kill—then, for the last time, he carries out the movement and gives himself into the Father's hands.

It is very clear that two different movements mingle here, the intrinsic movement of sacred life into the light and the great "being done" of the divine will, into whose remote and mysterious movement life enters at a particular point. Life experiences this movement as a power which changes its direction. By surrendering and yielding itself life may take part in the eternal movement. But here the mystery remains that even the movement of life into the light receives its goal and impulse from God.

Our plan signifies this spiritual casting-form. For the divine service this form means that individual and people enter into the eternal casting movement at a particular instant of their history, thence letting themselves be borne into a radiant place, but that there they are taken over into the backward flow and are cast again toward a borderline—toward a borderline which in turn makes its entrance at a particular point. The altar is once more the place of sacrifice, of the sacrifice of their own hope. The entire course lying between portal and portal is sacred movement and within it the altar marks the spot where the people relinquish their journey into the light. There they are taken into the vision of the Lord who yields himself to the dark will of the Father. At the beginning the building is directed to the altar but later on it is not the altar but the portal which points the way, which is the place of the second passing over, of the passing over into death.

Consequently the entire movement of the building is made up of two processes: of the great process of eternity and of the historical movement which enters into it. That bit of path common to both is "sacred way." It consists of an ascending part and a declining part, of a proceeding and a receding. At its beginning and at its end stands the portal. The portal at the end has a double meaning; and even in its meaning as gateway of eternity it is filled with the ambiguousness of the judgment: here blackness is separated from darkness.

In recent decades the projectile curve has often been used for the cross-section or ground-plan of new churches. Probably this occurred less out of a clear perception than out of a certain vague and general feeling in which the Gothic's heavy sense of approaching death awoke once more. This may have resulted from the influence of certain painters and their feeling for space or, too, it may have resulted from the experiences of the time. Men loved that vaulting which shoots up fountain-like out of the earth and, leaving a dark and melancholy space behind, turns over in a high crown. Still more they loved the more Gothic form of the arch which comes together in an acute angle, its two sides like two great inclined weights which plunge toward each other and mutually prevent one another from falling. The parabola is indeed an especially noble structural form, for, entirely self-contained and devoid of the least heaviness, it is the consummate form of the arch. Yet it was not loved for these things but simply for the mood it created; and men loved the Gothic form too, although the method of construction, this loyal protectress of the spirit of the times, did not produce it. But the feeling which brought forth these works could not endure for long since it was largely determined by the destiny of death suffered by the people in the last war, a destiny which, despite all bitterness, was short. And so this feeling disappeared as soon as life grew green again over the ruins. The few genuine works remained monuments to this time but the form itself deteriorated into simple motif and soon came into the wrong hands. Inasfar as these buildings are the fruits of real poetry one assents to them gladly. Their broad openness and their radiant lighting upward into the dome were developed logically out of the meaning of the figure. They would have had more future if their meaning had been more deeply understood and more profoundly considered and if it had then been given form steadfastly and with ever-growing clarity.

We must go back to medieval times in order to experience what it really means when people hold out year after year in a growing disaster into which they have been led, not by simple ill-luck, but by the true movement of eternity.

Every historical interpretation is difficult; all too willingly do we place our own time and its thought in a past which lived and thought differently and which perhaps did not even rightly understand itself. With this reservation, we believe that we see mounting in the buildings of the Middle Ages the growing alarm about the final things.

Some have wished to derive the early cathedrals from the idea of the "processio": in solemn succession portal, nave and altar journeyed across the earth. This idea remains correct for the Romanesque buildings—they are measured, marching procession, solemn entry of a holy people into its country. The golden apsis opens wide and solemnly the nave draws near to it. Even for the basilicas of late antiquity this idea holds true. Twice on the high walls in Ravenna we find the procession pictured—the pictorial progress accompanies the procession of the people. Out of the ancient apses the Saviour looks in deep earnestness out to the solemn procession. In his eyes the way back is already in the making. Here our second image is represented: the Lord sits at the Last Supper.

This image is still true for the Gothic. The majestic naves, going their radiant way from portal to altar, are a solemn progress. But already in them the fateful form of the cast is slowly emerging. The ribs draw together out of the arches, in the upper walls the divisions and articulations disappear, a single line of tension runs uninterruptedly over responders and ribs, leading the cast from the ground up into the apex and from the apex down again to the earth.

And then the divisions within the train of the "processio" begin to disappear. The triumphal arch, which once set an end to the train, falls away and the whirlpool at the intersection of transept and nave smooths out. Even in its ground-plan the High Gothic choir is nothing but the loop which comes into being when one great wall veers around into the other. A double casting-movement streams about the central nave, the space of the nave itself is flowing back—the spatial advance is drawn into a form which is pointing it backward. Nothing is left of the star-form found in the early apses. Now, like the column in the ancient arena, the altar is the spot where the curve turns.

All this becomes very clear in the flanking aisles. The side aisle is no longer a reflection of the nave to each side, no longer a train going with shorter steps beside the main procession, but rather a double stream which breaks in at the side portals, flows forward beside the nave, circles its end,

and then flows back again to the other portal. What began simply as a movement at the very edges of the nave becomes a space which men can tread.
What happens here is not a progress but a circuit, a casting which moves
solemnly around the altar at its apex and which then comes to an end again

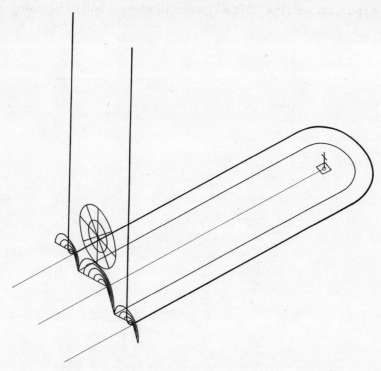

in the same condition in which it began, as remote from the altar as in the
beginning. But the meaning of the *direction* in which the west wall is pierced
changes; at the beginning the movement led out of the world and at the end
it leads back into it once more. Yet the movement never really reaches its
goal: it was near to it yet it passed it by.

Out of infinite space a second movement plunges down onto the first, as
spire. This second movement unites itself with the first, takes up the people
at the portal, describes the loop on the earth, sets the people down again at
the other portal and, as second spire, departs from the earth into infinite

space once more. At the same time it loses its spatiality once again: the passage which men could tread turns into a process of matter alone.

Still more majestic is the representation given the endless curve in Strassburg, where a single path soars from the altar out through the nave and up into the spire, or, seen the other way around, where a bolt of lightning strikes.

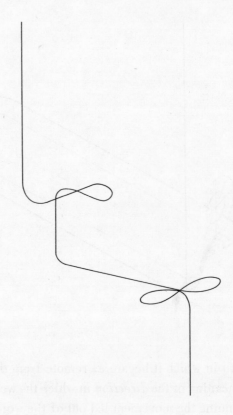

Thus the end of the Middle Ages stands wholly under the sign of the final things. The Saviour is executed on the high altar. He hangs alone in his final agony. Hell's revolt has broken loose, cracks and craters gut the earth and the infernal powers are escaping. This is shown us in Isenheim. In the neighboring cathedral at Breisach the Lord himself judges. This latter is the work of an artist very closely related to the Isenheim master. On the west side he joins onto the church a broad house and fills it from top to bottom with the Last Judgment. The burning bodies of the falling have turned to torches, causing the conflagration of the universe which stands in flame from the earth up to the very roof. On the other side, the trains of the blessed are climbing up over green and shimmering slopes into the cool and tranquil blue, led on by God's great messengers. Directly over the portal the Eternal King separates and judges, and he is the same Lord who is executed at the high altar. Here the second meaning of the portal emerges. It becomes clear that, far beyond the circumstance that this is the portal into the world, it is the gateway of eternity. Here the apsis is given its frightful counterpart— and the latter predominates. In the divine service the people go at first to the altar, they see the Lord's death before them but they know that his second coming is at their back. And even structurally the way which they must later travel to return back from the altar is the more important: the way into judgment, into damnation, into bliss.

Perhaps the masters of the earlier cathedrals, long before this late period, thought nothing of it when they took the judgment and the rose-window, this radiant image of the new earth which hovers high over the place of judgment, and put them, not at the head of the church, but at the entrance. But if this was the case, that sacred wisdom which inspired their work took care itself that this work turn out rightly. Afterward it was often said that these buildings are turned the wrong way round since they make the entrance more important than the choir. And this is true, too, for when we look to the end the familiar image of the earth becomes frightfully distorted: here the altar stands beside the way and the last things stand revealed at the end.

The means with which the Gothic erected its great curves flowing out into the infinite are bound to their own period and we have progressed beyond them. This particular art of building gathers all of its material together to render arches of function which, laden with tremendous powers, carry out an incredibly rapid movement. Here we sense the young functionalism for which life ceases to be "being" and begins to become "casting." Soon this functionalism will make of the earth a little star journeying through the universe, which falls into the sun, catches itself up again and with the same haste plunges back into the universe once more.

Like every true form, this form springs from a sacred source. Every new creature of this earth comes straight from the hand of God: he is the inventor of everything really new. (Parenthetically we may mention that the profound meaning of all church building is just this: to find, beyond all preliminary tasks, the absolute task and to introduce in incorrupted works the primal process itself, God's sacred maintaining of the world. Like the mystic who seeks the way to that innermost cell where God lives in the midst of the world, so the cathedral builder seeks to do God's true work, to render the process of all processes. Here in purity God's work should "be done.")

Sacred source of this functionalism is the anguish of uncertain salvation. Man sees that the earth is gloriously ordered, but he also sees that there is an open gap in the smooth ring of necessity and that he himself has been placed in this gap together with his own salvation. The ordering of the world does not guarantee that he will attain to it. This becomes clear to him and he is filled with alarm. He sees that he is alone and that his salvation in eternity is uncertain. He wants to hide himself in God, yet he finds that God withdraws out of the things. And then he goes to seek him. Out of the stuff of this world he forges an infinite curve, a hair-line bridge to bear him to God. Thus he loses his home yet even so he does not win heaven. This linear asceticism refines the stuff of this world but does not change it. The curve does not reach into heaven.

In those days most of the people left this work. They deserted an undertaking without promise and without a way of escape and they returned to the ground, taking with them the ascetic discipline. They became adventurers and discoverers of the universe. They subdued the inner realms of the cosmos; and yet in spite of all they remained despairing monks. Their way became an endless journey within the world and the structure of their world became a form of despair. The "dynamic" new world became a form of simple drivenness. That which really took place appeared only by intimation. Without his wishing it or expecting it a new meaning revealed itself to man on his way: simple enactment has an inner meaning as form. And indeed the world responded to the new forms, yet that which came into being was essentially abortive. Had mankind held out in its anguish the new world would assuredly not have become such a wild and terrible undertaking.

But perhaps the people's final desertion of the Lord belongs to the meaning of this movement, too, and perhaps they were still true to him as they went away. Those last who held out gathered together their dead memories and, as their last work, built of them the Pietàs where Mary weeps over a dead form. And at the very, very end, against all expectation, the Lord blessed the emptiness.

For us the language of the Gothic is outmoded. This carrying out of curves in their infinitude had an eternal meaning, the meaning that this infinity was a theological one and that little by little the world flowed into God.

We feel this in a different way. For us, all paths ultimately come together to form the rim of the world. Every movement flows back into itself and remains imprisoned in the universe. To continue the lines into their mathematical infinitude does not provide us with a way out—it leads us ever and again to the infinite rim. And hence it is for us the very means of experiencing the world centripetally as that creature which rests in the hand of God. The newly-won boundary reacts back onto the things. Our world is always and everywhere at an end and everywhere God is beyond it. We can carry out the world's movement to the very boundary—this the Gothic could not do. By yielding ourselves into the inner falling away of a limited form toward its rim, we can carry through the infinite movement to its very end, almost to God—and this we achieve within the pure restraint of a well-defined figure.

For us the functionalism of the Gothic has no theological meaning and in the end this functionalism must retreat; only then, in resignation, does it find God. Therefore our world is becoming flat once more. The lines of function, spreading out into fields, pour out their centrifugal force within the limited. Nor is this limitedness deeply hidden, for the negation has assumed a sort of omnipresence and lies manifest on the surface. Our world has become flat and spacious once more, yet this is no longer the quiet measuredness of Antiquity—rather is it a region full of hidden processes, full of a constant trickling, full of tensions, the region of constant creation and of constant headlong plungings into nothingness. That the form stands is no longer the natural thing but only a token for the fact that the struggle within it still "stands." Our world has become symmetrical again, but its symmetry is no longer that of an image reflected around an axis, rather is it the balance of forces which bind and brace one another.

Therefore the plan as we gave it at the beginning is, for today, the more genuine form of the eternal concern: the movement of eternity draws round the space in the majestic cast of the wall and the people move slowly into its openness; they are coming as if from the sea into harbor, its mouth lying at

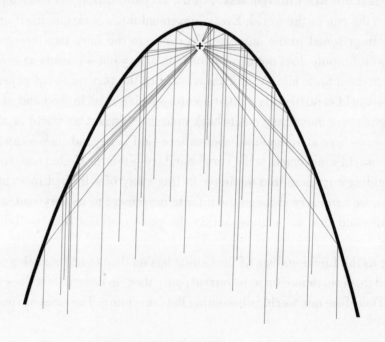

their back. (Here the similarity to the second plan appears again, for here, too, a way is joined to an open, concave form. But at the beginning everything is in reverse: here the way moves into the concavity whereas before it took leave from it—the form points back, the way points ahead. Thus the image of this movement is very difficult: the procession enters into a concave form which is itself carrying out a great backward-flowing movement.)

The constant movement of the figure out into its openness can be imagined in various ways.

We can conceive of it as a constant streaming forth of the space and of the space's delimitation out into the openness.

Or we can conceive of it as a double cast. Two casts pass around the focal point, one running from the left over to the right, the other from the right over to the left. This point is the early anchor of movements which come out of the infinite and then return into it once more, winning in the focal point their single bond with the ground, the place where they are anchored in the finite.

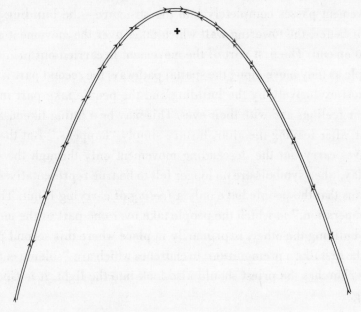

We can also imagine that it is the casting movement which engenders the focal point. The curve enters the focal point and then goes forth out of it, now translated into space—as space the boundary unfolds itself out of this point as if out of a sprouting seed. This point would be the place where space and surrounding wall were translated into each other. The particular course of the boundary directs the lengthwise movement of the space into this spot. Then, gathered together there, the entire inner space is taken up into the backward-flowing movement of the boundary.

Lastly we may also imagine that the inner space streams forward following the central axis and that from the apex it then flows back on the outside. This again produces the motion of the fountain, of the column of water which, in falling, turns over to encase itself and thus nourishes its bounds from its own substance.

All these concepts work the people into a more exalted whole in which man and building play their parts together. The people tread only the spatial part of this architectural work, that which lies between door and altar. Then the movement passes completely into the structure—the building bears it alone, or better, the towering wall which takes over the movement and carries it to an end. The first part of the movement is carried out primarily by the people as they move along the spatial pathway, the second part is carried out almost exclusively by the building and the people take part in it only with their feelings and with their eyes. This may be a fitting likeness for the fact that, after leaving the altar, history simply "happens." But the people themselves carry out the descending movement only through the symbol. And today, when symbols are no longer felt to be true representatives of life, this means that the people have only a *feeling* of carrying it out. Therefore this "cooperation," in which the people take over one part of the movement and the building the other, is primarily in place where this second part embraces the first like a premonition: in churches which are "solemn entrance." In these churches the priest should also look into the light, it is God's near dwelling.

Yet this has already changed in churches which are "Last Supper." The crisis is drawing near. One might think that the building would still continue to carry out the declining movement representatively; yet we believe that it is more correct if this movement, too, is introduced within the people themselves. It should first become manifest in the priest. As he bears the people's prayer through Christ to the Father, he stands in the shining spot, looking out toward them; his eyes pass back over the people, back into the emptiness behind the procession, back into the darkness. He turns all the prayers back and sends them into the open origin.

The final step is where the people themselves carry out both branches of the movement. Here, of course, we encounter the difficulty that all Christian religious building is to a certain degree static since it ties a process to a local habitation. The building must preserve this process in a standing form which carries out the movement inwardly. Thus "journey" was preserved as "way-ordering" and in the same way the casting movement is here consummated by an ordering in which the people look forward and the priest looks back. In earlier times the liturgy was richer in movement, but much of this has since died out. One movement, however, still remains, almost alone, the movement in which the people go to the Lord's table and then return from it. And in this one movement, irrevocable for all times, that is given which we are seeking here: way forward, union and way back. Usually little meaning is attributed to the second part of the movement. But it has a profound content: way into the end. Being sent away from the altar is ordinarily conceived of as being sent home, into the world, to our work. This is right. But profounder and more valid is its second meaning, that of being sent into darkness, into the last judgment, and of the supper providing food for this journey. This is the sacral meaning of the way back to the portal. If we wish to make this meaning clear—above and beyond its first representation which is actually rendered by the people in life—then we must bring the portal into prominence, and it must be made plain that, far above the circumstance that this is the doorway into the world, this portal is the place of judgment.

It is possible, even certain, that another time will find another form for its eternal care since the forms of the anguish of salvation change. But behind all the unique achievements which can never be repeated and which have become outmoded by the progress of history, behind all the shortcomings of our attempt to clarify history, the fact remains that in all these buildings the life of the spirit rendered itself as a flowing form with an ascending and a falling branch, that at the beginning this course leads into light, that it touches a brilliantly radiant place but cannot hold itself there and so falls back into darkness. The radiant point is only a passing episode in the whole course; heaven was touched for an instant and this touch was then taken along as food for the descent. At the beginning the light gave direction, and to go rightly one needed only to go toward it; but then the portal became the goal, the doorway, with all the ambiguous things portending in it. Yet even this declining branch is guided by the light as it casts the ever-longer shadows ahead. A last gift of the dividing light shows men the right way into death as it teaches them to follow the lesson which their own darkness gives.

In this form the light is not a blessed end and rest but only the passing by of the Lord, a moment of blissful hovering in clarity, and then solace and succour on the way into the growing darkness. And finally the right way runs to the very place where the earth is darkest. At the beginning this way seemed to be the way home, but the friendly way becomes sinister and the end is in question. The direction toward the goal of the sacred way has reversed itself frightfully—it leads into judgment, and darkness goes ever at its side. At the beginning it had seemed as if the darkness would be conquered; but what seemed to be victory was comfort, was prelude to the final, deferred decision. The danger is growing, it was too early for the victory. What remains trustworthy is the food which this radiant memory provides, and the lesson which comes from it—and its promise, too: high over the portals in the west hovers the new creation, a burning rose, pledge of the Father's sacred love.

This is what remains as the intended form:

The life of the spirit: a cast into death. A form of anguish, and also a form of existence thought out to the very end and of sacred way carried out to the very end. Certainly not everyone is charged to live in this form. But he who has reached this ultimate insight is not free to choose whether he will acknowledge it or not. He must decide whether to hold out with the Lord in the everlasting agony of the dark chalice which the Lord must forever drink, or whether, despairing, he will fall back into the dumb fear of the animals in which the gloom of undivided darkness abides.

Sacred Universe
The Dome of Light

THE SIXTH PLAN shows the world made round again and the people united once more about the center. Thus from the very end of time this plan replies to the beginning of time. It fulfills and explains the very first plan. At the beginning, history was sealed in the seed and at the end, out of history, ripens the round and golden fruit. The beginning has been consummated.

Once again the rings of the people close, once again the world forms its vault. But this time it is a dome of sheer light. The building consists of light, light breaking in from all sides, light shining forth from all things, light fused with light, light turning to face light, light the answer to light. The earth is transformed into a star, her stuff afire, she is a monstrance of rays about the child in the center, her altar a flame, the people a sea of fire and each one of them a star. All the land and all the nations spread out without end within the universe. The vault of the world is a pellucid infinitude, clear and transparent like an evening sky high in the mountains, ethereal and incorporeal, a golden effulgence where the heavenly beings are hovering

180

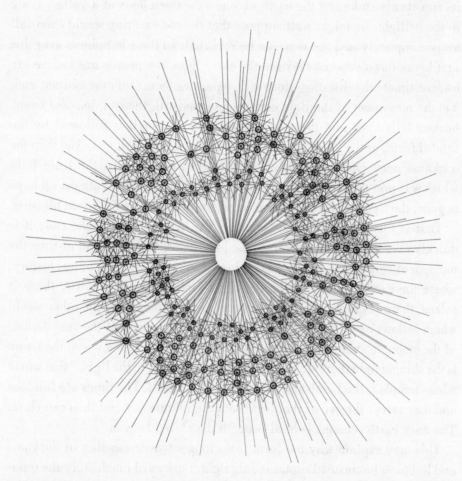

motionless in bliss. Heaven is everywhere, earth everywhere, the one melting into the other.

The eternal joy comes at a late time when it is no longer hoped for and it comes, not in a gradual development, but in a flash. At the very beginning when the closed form breaks open and light falls into the darkness this joy seems near. And when, through the world's "window," the vista into the eternal light opens up, it may seem as if the darkness would now begin to be gradually consumed. Or when the vaulting tears open at the crown, when its rim slowly sinks and the earth becomes the open floor of a valley, lying in the twilight, we might well suppose that the old vaulting would soon fall away completely and the new one be revealed. In their happiness over this first break-through when they see the early light, the people are inclined to underestimate the distance which still separates them from the radiant end. Yet the movement of the light comes to a standstill, the end does not come, heaven falls back and the first radiant break-through is followed by the fateful forms of the journey and the casting back into darkness. And then the darkness must close over once more, swallowing up even the little light which was present in the early beginning, until finally, when almost all hope is gone, the light is of a sudden at hand, an unawaited gift, a late blessing.

That is the joyous vision at evening, the blessed state at the end; it is quickly over and afterward comes the long night. Until the end of time the moment of epiphany is short. Where this moment emerges out of our history, where the earth betrays her hidden light-form, there is promise, there is solace, there is grace. And this moment is ever a pledge of the other world which follows after ours, that world which "has no need of the sun, neither of the moon, to shine in it: for the eternal light doth lighten it and the Lamb is the shining light thereof, and the nations shall walk in the light," that world whose temple is the Lamb and God Almighty himself. The times are fulfilled and they tarry; the eye of the world sees the infinite joy and then can close. The dark earth remains behind beneath the closed heaven.

This may explain why the form is no longer woven together of darkness and lightness but instead contains only light. Backward into history the inter-weaving is present. The infinite radiance of the form is bought at the price of the abysmal darkness which preceeded it. The previous plan ended without light; both belong together and the movement which they share completes what happened deep in the final threshhold at the very end of the way-form. For the last time it is true that emptiness calls forth fullness, the utter dark-ness pure light. The holy earth has suffered her final anguish, has died and been carried to the tomb, and God the Almighty and the Good awakens her and she climbs from the grave arrayed in shining raiment.

The end-form itself is no longer a process since in it time stands still. It is one single glorification, a song of praise, the unalloyed existence of joy. The wedding of the Lamb is at hand and the bride is attired in radiant white.

This structure may also be called a dome, yet it is no longer a vault which walls a cave but rather that ball which is the primal form of light, the sphere. A part of the idea of this design is that it extends endlessly, but each of the innumerable concentric balls in which the light dilates is itself a sort of vault. This plan is eternal vaulting, vaulting of light, and in this it is the answer to the very first plan which was vaulted of darkness. These are the only two legitimate forms of the dome and where the dome is to succeed it must be vaulted in accordance with one of these two plans: either as the dark casing about the radiant bud of the center or as the endless openness of light itself. Where we realize this plan in a building we will render a single one of the concentric balls of light, but the material for this representation must be light itself: it should be like a single apsis following in the wake of one of the innumerable balls of light. Here we could repeat everything which we said in the second plan about the building of the apsis and in the third about the building of the radiant dome. The ways of realizing this plan are varied but they all mean the same thing: that the world is lying in the eternal light.

Perhaps we may say that true eternal vaulting has thus far been genuinely successful only in the north where the Gothic, too, succeeded and where the sacred movement was carried through into the final agony. What drove the southern Renaissance to the dome was not the longing for the "heavenly city," for the "eternal Jerusalem," but rather a humanistic way of looking at things. They wanted the consummate measure, the monument of the free human being and thus at bottom they wanted the structure of a new world-cave. The Roman paganism attempted the arch once again—the form which had been shattered for them a thousand years before—and after a century of vain attempts, this humanism which was no humanism had to be returned

into the form of man as he really is. Even Bramante's plan, which miscarried
so magnificently, was humbled into the way-form. The Italian vaulting took

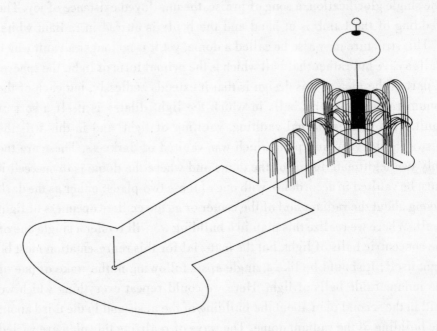

on the Baroque form of the nave, the form in which the central dome stood
only at the nave's end, and thus they returned to the truth and to faith, to the
very place where the Gothic had ended.

In its dreams of the sacred centric structure which it never achieved the
Gothic had never longed for the humanistic cave. This would have been easy
—too easy. What the Gothic wanted, what it sought and what was forever
denied it (denied it in a very meaningful way: Gothic technology, which
otherwise produced the most astonishing results, was at a loss here) was infinite openness in all directions, world built of the "streaming light of the
Divinity." And yet this sacred cathedral was never achieved. The building
miscarried because in a profound sense it could not succeed—God refused
to grant it. Only much later did that joy come and it came in a form which
has rightly been called a transformed Gothic. In Neresheim, in the Church of

the Fourteen Saints, the radiant vault came true as the horizon of eternity about the golden altar in the center. The saints throng about it, and round about the dome overhead they are present once more. The eye forces its way out through their sphere, out through ever more distant, ever greater spheres, out into the "open heaven." The heaven within and the heaven round about respond to one another, and what remains of the earth, the walls at the edge of the space, are clad in bridal white.

The East, too, achieved the eternal dome. Byzantine church building shows the world become one single house of God outside of which nothing else exists. The dome is the outermost sphere of light and there God is enthroned in his glory. The blessed vision of the world in her final state never departed from this building. It preserves the moment of epiphany as a memory and as a pledge up until the final day when the eternal city will come down to earth. But since in these buildings the moment of bliss was turned to lastingness they stand at the side of history and at the side of its commandment to "work as long as it is day." The Eastern churches are like monks whose lives are consecrated to the vision of God. This is their incomparable glory and also the reason why, in the end, they perished.

PART III
The Seventh Plan

The Cathedral of All Times
The Whole

SIX PLANS have grown up, one after the other. Each of them contained a history which, over a succession of forms, brought forth the abundant grace of the end-form. The historical process was stilled to condition in the structure of each plan, yet each plan could be read backward into time. And at bottom it was ever the same history, the history of that sacred people which goes to God, called and led by his grace until they reach the "threshhold" where the earth fails them; the history of the "sacrifice" they bring when, having exhausted all earthly possibilities and having realized that all their labors were in vain, they leave everything to God; the history of the superabundant grace which guides the forms of devotion and which rewards the sacrifice; the history of the new world which comes back out of eternity across the threshold. This same sacred history came to pass in each of the plans. It ran through each of them and the world was created anew. Thus God's own most intrinsic work was rendered in the "plans," the work of all works, the history of all histories.

Thus six plans of the world's creation yielded themselves. They showed the world in differing images: as "ring," then as "open ring" and as "chal-

189

ice" in the two forms of the early "parting," then as "way," then as "cast" and finally once again as "ring." But the natural world, given under whatever sign, did not suffice—it could not find its fulfillment in its own meaning, it needed the divine completion. Therefore these plans were founded in grace, which renews the dissolving forms, and therefore they were made whole in God who closes the gaping form. "Heaven" was an element of the plans, or more correctly we would have to say the "place of heaven," for heaven itself remained "beyond" them and had ever to be sought at the place where they themselves remained unfinished and "open."

And at the side of each design stood its temptation, a form of despair: the round form hardened in itself, the cave, the empty journey—the forms of dumb fear into which the world degenerates when it attempts to establish itself in its own meaning and to carry out autonomously the movement of history. And so these worlds perpetually faced decline or ruin and had ever to be renewed in constant sacrifice.

The world was placed in the landscape of eternity where the great eternal movement flowed through it and the sight of the eternal places gave it direction. The natural form of the universe was the bearer of an eternal meaning. An eternal sun illumined the spiritual landscape and creation turned to this sun in her prayer. The natural structure of the world and the movement of life toward the natural sun became the likeness of an eternal universe. There is meaning in the fact that God designed the world as it is and not otherwise. God erected this world in accordance with the plan of eternity and even in the primeval cult of the sacred sun there is truth.

Here two things may seem strange.

For one, that the eternal landscape has form and delineation at all.

There is little that we can reply to this. The eternal landscape could, of course, be different, it could be amorphous. But it is not and of this a thousand witnesses give evidence. Only our own thinking has become amorphous and we must orient it once more to the compass of eternity and nourish our mind in the clarity of eternity's form.

And then it seems strange that there are several forms of the spiritual world. It would be simpler to think either that there is only one structural form of this cosmos or that there are an infinite number. But it is hard to understand that there should be a certain precisely determined number of such world plans, no more and no less. All this seems governed by the law of chance.

If we pursue the question we find a profound inner order in the apparently so accidental collection of "plans." They do not stand as independent entities but are built upon each other and toward each other and they open up into each other. What began in a previous one is continued in the next and what happens in a later one is prepared in an earlier one. Each plan is self-contained form but is built in such a way that it evokes a second form. Each "plan" enters transformed into the next through the portal which it made ready for its own passage.

A single movement flows uninterruptedly through all the "plans" and one of its phases is set down in each of them. We can follow each element through all the plans and if we do this we find that through them all and beyond them all each element carries out one great, single movement. This is true for the people and their changing forms as well as for the forms of the earth or the universe and it is even true for the most holy place: the "sun" of these worlds, too, travels a great course and each plan shows one of its positions. But since each of the plans deals with the way the earth moves toward the eternal sun, the great history which is consummated here across all the "plans" is a solar history. The eternal light travels its own path, and the world follows in its wake; the beautiful, delicate movement in the "natural" world, which is made daily by all living things in answer to the path of the sun, is clarified spiritually in this supra-natural heliotropism.

In the "plans" we discover the elements of a succession of forms.

We encountered the linking of forms into a logical sequence when we spoke about the growth of plants which brings forth one form after another and grows to fulfillment through a succession of phases. Such a "succession" is built in such a way that each of its forms is wholly self-contained, complete within its own meaning, yet just because it is as it is, it requires that another form, and a very particular one, follow after it. Each form is pre- or post-determined by the others, but not like question and answer which complete each other, nor like sisterly forms which can be interchanged, nor like pairs of forms in which a whole is built up of two parts, but rather in the same way that different parts of a meaningful course belong to each other: one and the same substance passes through changing phases.

The plans are bound by a living bond. This bond is historical time. We may imagine the plans strung along it. Then a sort of spectrum comes into being within which each plan has its own particular "place." Sometimes a phase spreads out over a wide stretch of the spectrum, at other times, where the great decisions come and event crowds fast on event, the segment is set thick with forms. But since each plan is itself built up out of a succession of forms—we illustrated this from time to time—the segment of spectrum which it occupies may be further subdivided by registering these different phases. Some parts of the "spectrum" are then like broad stripes within which the coloring changes very slowly and some are like fine spectral lines; these latter mark the swift changes.

We are already acquainted with this pattern, too—it means history: the great movement of living time which enters into one period after another, then to hurry through it and depart. Little by little one space of time is strung to the next to form the whole. Across all phases, a higher order of history, the true history, is accomplished. And across all phases a form of a higher rank is revealed, the true form. In the course of time a composite form emerges: the whole becomes visible and our plans are contributions to it—limbs of the greater body.

Here is the course of this great history:

At first the things lie in quiet harbor about their center, turned completely to the inside. Then in the crown above or at some point on the perimeter a source of light begins to make itself felt. The closed form splits open, what had been safely sheltered is cleft and the figure discharges into the openness. The space takes leave of the form and journey begins. The powerful ascent at the beginning gradually tires as it reaches the dead point in the apex, then opposing forces come into play and finally the movement comes to a standstill. The counteraction prevails. The movement feels itself checked and thrown back, it hesitates, time stands still and at the point where the movement came to rest new space unfolds out of the distended figure. A new center has come into being and new world is gathered about it in a new sphere.

How obvious is the comparison to plant life, which constantly accompanied us, and how obvious, too, the comparison to the human life and its story and even to the life of the Lord! And these comparisons are right for they show how life's history is built, how it is constructed of a definite number of periods, each of which possesses a definite form, and they show how the sequence of these forms gradually brings forth the "other body"—that body which life slowly creates along the time-ordinate and which also has a form of its own. Thus each of the six plans represents a space of time within the great world-history of the sacred and this history itself, woven between eternity and eternity, possesses then its own great, clear form. The sequence of the plans was established not by accident but rather by the very structure of creation itself—and this is indeed not an accident, it is the revealed form of eternity in time.

Our seventh "plan" is the composite form of the sacred history—within it the first six plans are only limb, period and phase. Three great elements go to make it up. The first and the last are centric and between them the way takes its course. Where it leaves the one centric form and where it flows into the other arise situations of transition, situations of departure and of homecoming. Like two open harbors the two end-forms turn to face each other, one the port of putting out to sea, the other that of putting into harbor, and between them stretches the path of life: this is the form at the root of the sacred history. The whole form present at one time is once more like a tree, with its crown of roots buried in the darkness, its trunk, and its crown of branches in the light.

That building which summons all phases into structure ot once, uniting time's entire flow within itself, is the cathedral of all times. Age-old it

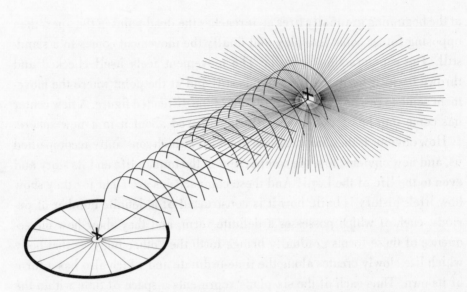

towers over the epochs and in uniting them to one great form it adds something new which none of them had possessed, not even the last: the completion, the whole. The cathedral possesses the fullness of time. It gathers the phases together and, overcoming them, it welds them all into that higher form which towers above all epoch and which lies at the heart of all and which is yet more than all. In this cathedral time comes to its end. The cathedral's form is held out into eternity. The cathedral sends no world back into her history. It stands finished in the quiet of the seventh day and the eye of God rests upon it. Its form is the form of time's boundary and the outline of eternity. Its contours circle all epoch, they trace the outline of history as it stands neither this side of time nor beyond it, rising in silhouette against the timeless—transient, dissolving forms. Transition or "threshhold" is no longer to be found at this particular point or that, it is all about: everywhere along the rim time is merged with the eternal. This form no longer means "sacrifice," the world being led to her rim by an eternal light. Rather does it mean the completion and then the dissolution of time. God passes through the structural form and in following after him the peoples erect the form of the cathedral; in it, they consummate time, and God is present.

Only the cathedral is true body. The plans were like limbs of the hidden body of history; they contained the whole by implication but they themselves remained its phase. One plan dwelt in the other, each dwelt in all and in each the whole. Even in the ring, at the very beginning, parting, journey, death and the new closure at the end were present; in the ring the way was already prepared for the opening movement, the darkness at the back of the world was already at hand and even the ultimate solitude was present, just as a last comradeship remained in the rigorous way-form and just as, at the very end, that form itself was seen to be nothing else but a tiny piece of the infinite ring. In each of the six plans the others are present either as memory or as foreshadowing. Each one of them tends toward the whole but they are themselves only the organ which is used to serve it and which then rests once more. A higher life is at hand and it speaks from time to time in changing forms. But that which speaks is ever present. It could be called "the church."

In the cathedral, however, all limbs are joined together. The cathedral is like the human body which also gathers all times and conditions into itself as eye, as hand, as foot. Each of these organs takes part in the whole: as eye, the whole gives answer to light, as foot it becomes way through space, as hand, surface. When the action moves into another organ the first relaxes and is still, but it remains bound into the whole by the coursing of the blood. In the cathedral, which is history become present, coursing flow gathered into structural form, the bodily likeness is complete for the first time. The action moves now into this one of the cathedral's spaces, now into that, according to the seasons, and, when the action sleeps in the other spaces, this one awakens into time. Time passes through the cathedral in the same way that the days and years flow through the branches of an age-old tree which unfurls its leaves, moves them a little, covers itself with blossoms and fruit and yet through all this scarcely changes except that very slowly it grows old.

Therefore this seventh is a plan above all plans and no one man can build it. For he would stand within his own period, his building would show its meaning and everything else would be hidden within this. Our architecture with its comparative permanence corresponds to the period. But the seventh plan lays the epochs end to end into one great form, and its walls are the horizon of eternity.

Therefore our thinking must be reborn.

At no time in history can the last plan be completely realized but in many varied ways it shines through the architecture of the epochs, showing itself now in this way, now in that. The "whole" is to be discovered in one thing above all others: in the act of the divine service. Indeed, this act builds itself up along the time-ordinate and its form, brought forth in the flow of time, is in a sense the "whole." Each time, this sacral work builds, through the movements of its inner space, through its climbing and falling, through its swelling and ebbing, the cathedral of all times.

The "whole" also becomes visible in the flow of the church year, for of course the form of the year is erected along the time-axis, too. Period by period, in the changing forms of Christmas, Easter and Pentecost, the cathedral is gradually erected.

Thirdly, each new day erects the whole. For each morning is a parting and each evening brings home a harvest and the sun rounds her course from night unto night.

And, lastly, we can even say the same thing of every breath, for it, too, is an entering and a departing and has its profound meaning.

Thus the sacred whole is constantly happening and yet it cannot be captured in any work of architecture for the meaning of architecture is permanency and not transformation. Time is taken out of the stream of events and made solid in architecture—the great structure looks quietly out over the changing process. The art of building is not allied with the short transformations of breathing, of the act of worship, of the course of the day or year, nor with the great course of history from eternity to eternity. It corresponds only to the age. Architecture stresses the meaning at the heart of the epoch, quiets its movement and erects it in great structure. As if out of a remoteness devoid of time, walls and vaulting look down on the act of worship, thus enclosing their own space in ultimate crystallization. And so two kinds of space are interwoven in this great building: the flowing space of the action is

embedded in the immutably fixed space of the great architectural structure—
space becomes the container of space. Life runs its course in an architectural
landscape—the stage remains whereas the action changes. One of its own
periods gives shelter to the whole.

Structure as Play of Light

If we want to render this whole and not the epoch, without waiting for the
aging of world history which builds space onto space and finally completes
the cathedral, then we must relinquish the usual means of architecture. We
must look about for a new and more flexible instrument. If we could also
succeed in making the *inner* spatiality of a process visible, if we could make
the building run parallel to the action, then the ingenious interweaving of
two spatial forms, which is today such an important law of all building,
would vanish. The space would be utterly at one. In the theater this has been
partially achieved, particularly in opera, where the action spreads about it
a powerful area of sound and where the scenery, too, changes frequently.
(Here a certain disunity still remains between the scenery and the action
since the scenery is always a stage, if not for the entire play, then at least for
one "scene," and thus the scenery lives within a space of time which is longer
than that within which the action lives. But the magical transformations of
scene on open-air stages in the midst of the performance, which distinguish
this play-space from the natural landscape in an important way, may perhaps mean that we are beginning to overcome this disunity—particularly
since they are furthered by our modern technique of projection onto a va-
cant "shell.")

What the theater has begun could be further developed and the whole
"stage" for the act of worship could be set in motion. We possess the technical means for rendering such changing spaces of light and the fact that we
have them may prove that the old conceits of architecture are in dissolution.
Perhaps this new architecture will make it possible for man to create his
universe ever anew, just as the techniques of "traffic" have enabled him to
move freely in space.

It is conceivable that in the future our churches may come into being solely out of the act of worship itself. At the beginning there would be no space and at the end none would be left over. The space would come into being and would sink away simultaneously with the service. The act of worship is indeed a spatial process whose "processio" is bound to a fixed spot, and as a "processio" of spatial transformation it could be unfolded *out* of this spot: the altar. What the ancient religious buildings achieved by the transition from one space into another would here be accomplished by the transformation of space welling forth from within. In connection with the second plan we mentioned a proposal which was intended in this way. At bottom this would complete what the liturgy itself has already begun. Even today its space does not simply soar invisibly amongst the walls. The movements of the people, their changing position, the variation of the lighting, the solemn rhythms of the area of sound—all these together render that process which is the liturgy. It would be only a final step to give up the fixed structural space entirely and to use the structure simply as a means with which to render, in free creation, the ever-changing space. Then the liturgy would not only be a "cathedral" in its secret structure: every day the Whole would be visibly erected.

Structure as Vessel

Such thoughts are not at all remote from us today.

The profound meaning of the sacral act has come alive to us once more. For us, this act is again that which is real and important, and the building, too, should grow out of it. It has often been said that the building should be nothing more than a good instrument for the sacral act and that it should anticipate nothing of that which God creates and calls into life only in this act itself. The world should, as it were, be led back before the first day of creation and then be created anew "out of nothing." This creation should take place in living men, not in images and buildings—at the beginning the building should be simply the means of this creating and afterward the result of it.

Many of our new churches have been left almost entirely without images. They clearly confess their "emptiness" in the costly but abstract decoration of windows and in the noble but plain form of their utensils. All this says that they are noble instruments for the act of worship but nothing more than that. Only in the divine service should the plain form of the instrument be raised to exalted reality. The space and its light should be created from within, as sacred achievement; even the altar, which in the beginning is only a table, should itself be created; that which was merely an earthly substance in the beginning should come into being as sacred body; and as the act of worship ends this creation should die away again—it should be consumed just as the consecrated species themselves become food for the journey. Everything is expressed in the idea that only as much bread and wine should be made ready as will be received, in order that the act of worship may end with an empty table. This holy world comes into being out of "nothing" and leaves "nothing" behind, God "passed by" and his grace has become food for men. Like each of God's sacred words the sacred species are food for the journey, and when they are stored up this happens in order that they may be consumed later on. The whole has come to pass. It was sown where the altar stands, it took root and grew tall, spreading out over all people, and then it died away once again.

But all this, right and beautiful as it is, has its limits and it becomes false when they are overstepped.

The concept of the "instrument" is one such limit.

Even assuming that it would be possible to keep all the things used for the holy service—the building itself, the altar, even the wording and the melody of the language—as a means, as an empty vessel, then this vessel would still be left over and it would have a form and this form would have a meaning. In the instrument, too, a meaning is stored away and this meaning does not lie in explanations nor in decorative additions; we can safely form the instruments out of their simple function and we should do so. But this function is not an end and the instruments are not means. This idea would lead into the void, "nothing" would result from it. In the end the church would exist as a machine for performing the liturgy, and would be as utterly empty and void as the "machine for living" which is so rightly mocked. These things are not intended to *serve* liturgy but to *be* liturgy, even if in a modest way. They are real things which are offered in sacrifice: the works of men.

The chalice is a drinking vessel: in the first place it is a vessel, a concave form into which we may pour a liquid, and hence it is a form needful of completion; secondly, it is a vessel for drinking and hence a form related to man, to his hand, his eye, his mouth; thirdly, it is God's holy blood which is drunk from it and thus the chalice is a form which is open to God—but it is a form made by man. And since it is as *form* that the chalice is related to all these things, it is itself something.

An extreme antithesis to the concept of the liturgical "instrument" was advocated by the monks of Beuron among others. They designed their chalices—which, for their time, were very beautiful—in accordance with formal ideas which were only remotely related to the use of the chalice. The monks gave them names such as "the wise Virgin" and thus they said that these things were creatures. Similar attempts have been made in our own times, as for instance when a chalice is assembled out of the elements of the empty sphere, the cylinder and the circular disk. Here the task is attacked very formally because an eternal meaning is suspected in the simplest forms.

We distrust such attempts because they are border-line cases. The truth lies within the area which they delimit. Instruments should be formed out of meaning and function at once—then beautiful, clear, basic forms arise which seek to be neither more nor less than chalices, candlesticks, a table, a book, a wall. They need not be utterly without adornment but their ornamentation should serve their meaning. A hanging lamp should above all show the flame which consumes the oil, a candlestick exists for the candle, a lectern for the book, the book for the writing and the writing for the reading.

Perhaps for us the building is in truth more vessel than edifice. But in that case the same applies to it which applies to the good vessel: the church building is like a "chalice." A meaning is stored up even in that building which is nothing more than an instrument and thus in it, too, the rapidly passing process is embedded in a lastingness which speaks into the building from out of its remoteness. The movement of the light is like the rapid transformation of the heavens at dawn and evening. But the firmament remains, just as the landscape and the mountain ranges and the valleys remain, in which the short life of man runs its course.

Even when the sacral act begins on a completely empty table, at least this table is already in existence, as is the earth on which it stands and the building which is to shelter the divine service—a whole world is already present and it is a sacred world since it stands for the living church which also is already present, even though she will be renewed in the sacrifice—a "house of God," a "rock," a "mighty fortress." The process of the sacred history is embedded in the everlastingness of the sacred presence, it takes place within the space of the already consummate redemption, and here the theological limit of this beautiful idea shows itself: the sacred history is both a task still to be done and a reality which is already complete.

All historical process is embedded in something durable even when this durable retires completely into the darkness. It may be beautiful and meaningful to think of the world as a becoming and a passing away, to raise it up out of the darkness and to let it run out again through the fingers; the world as "experience": emptiness at first and afterward only a swiftly vanishing footprint. But such thinking is an extreme. And therefore the idea that the sacred space arises and passes away together with the sacred act is an extreme, too. For indeed we cannot take the world back before her first morning and long ago God made ready the space in which we live. The Sacred as "God's passing by" is an extreme case and even though it may perhaps interpret the religious thought of the north in a legitimate way, it still remains at the extreme.

There is a second extreme case.

This is the belief that history is permanence, a gathering of great statues about which time blows like a gentle breeze. This conception may be at home in the East and in Antiquity, or it may stand everywhere at the side of the first one. There are things which show that the north, too, can think in this way: Meister Eckhart draws the image of the great mountain, standing immovable in a soft wind—a man should come to be like this, he says—and the sacred glades of the north were filled completely with the presence of the divine. The Greek temple served the sacred presence, the sacred image was enthroned in an inaccessible shrine. He who immersed himself for one night in this presence of Being became whole and inspired. The eastern churches are even today filled with the sacred, steeped in the palpable presence of God. Usually they are dark and almost without windows. As an area set apart the holy of holies lies behind the golden iconostasis whose images show the Saints in their final form, bathed in the golden ground and with the wide-open eyes of the beatific vision. Hanging lamps and candles illumine these pictures so that they become holy lights in holy darkness. Where, in the same neighborhood, a church of the western cult stands with her "emptiness," devoid of mystery in her sober obviousness, she cannot stand the comparison, even though she and her cult are also permeated by the faith in a sacred presence, by the faith in consecration and benediction, in sacred imagery and in sacred building and above all by the faith in the Lord's presence; nor is she conceived without a storing up of the sacred, and to her, too, the sacral act interweaves with the present, embedding change in permanence and "becoming" into being—it is only that she stands closer to the first extreme.

Thus we must always build the churches out of both of these elements and when one of them is lacking completely the churches miscarry. In this task there are two legitimate styles or forms. In the one, the space is unfolded almost completely out of the sacral act and that which is lasting remains entirely in the background. In the other that which is lasting becomes an edifice made spacious for life. It is conceivable that both ways of building be cultivated at once. The Ancients built the Athenian Parthenon as a shrine for a statue and at the same time they built the temple at Eleusis as a vessel

—this latter could even be partially transformed through the light. East and West could develop their different forms further, as valuable opposites. But we could also imagine buildings which would combine both elements, the shining, manifest "field of action" and the dark, hidden "shrine," the passage and the permanence of grace. Such buildings would perhaps consist of two rooms, one large, with the table in its center, the other small, containing the holy of holies. The ground-plan would have two poles and these would represent the eternal opposites in accordance with which the sacred history itself is also built. But, finally, lastingness and change could be united in the same space. Perhaps this would even be the best solution. It would not be wrong to make the altar into table and tabernacle at once, thus planting the sacred act into its own presence. The altar, the sacred earth, is Christ, too; this lasting rock bears the instruments of the act of worship. And even when the altar is empty it is the holy of holies in a church. Therefore it seems to us legitimate to build "shrine" and "table" into each other and to renew the creation of the world within the heart of the sacredly created world. It is of course also legitimate to separate the two places, for indeed we cannot actually divide "head" from "heart" in any case.

We must not forget that process and lastingness are primarily basic concepts of history, not of ritual. If they have a spiritual meaning then this means only that the divine has submitted to the law of time. The stuff of history tends to become fixed and to store itself up in a particular condition. In the midst of the flow some event or other steps forward, deposits itself and becomes lasting. This does not mean that it enters eternity—if eternity is understood to be that which it alone is, God's mode of being—rather does it step to the shore, so that later on it may become process once again. That which here becomes a condition was time and remains time. Nor does architecture have more to do with eternity than any other work. Architecture is lasting but it owes this lastingness to a favorable moment which deposited itself—and architecture lasts only in order to be let back into happening.

In the course of history process and lastingness are interwoven. Out of the living flow one phase rises up and makes itself into a work of architecture.

It steps aside and vaults itself over the happenings: that which clothes the process comes forth out of it, one of the process's own events becomes the period within which the process dwells. Of all the many things it contains, one becomes a work of architecture which shelters the happening.

Here we may perhaps be permitted to inject an idea which lies somewhat apart from our theme.

Is not the very question of the "storing up" of the consecrated species simply a part of this historical scheme? Is it not permissible to think that here a definite space of time within the act of worship, the heart of it, is stored up into condition? This condition then stands still, but it is not immortalized —that would indeed be to depreciate the act of worship which lives wholly in eternity—the condition is simply stored up as nourishment, as food to be consumed later on. And thus this has the same meaning as all historical storing up. The meaning of all storing up is "nourishment," not "immortalization." It would indeed be a poor eternity if the most banal things could be made fit for it, as poor as the poor endlessness of things which never want to end, like certain mathematical curves. Considered in this way, and assuming that this is a legitimate conception, then the meaning of the eucharistic storing up would be that the very heart is taken out of the sacred act and elevated to lastingness. In this way God's passing by and the sacred presence would be interwoven, one would proceed out of the other. And in this interweaving history's most intrinsic law would be taken up into the sacred.

We would like to illustrate the living interpenetration of process and lastingness with a few examples.

Once we were asked to give advice on the renovation of a church at a place of pilgrimage. As a result of its location and certain other circumstances this church bore a particular relationship to Saint Francis. Therefore on the back wall, behind the altar, the vicar wanted to represent that occurrence in which the Saint suffered the stigmata of the Lord. To us it seemed, however, that such an event, which could certainly be represented in a painting, was not monumental enough to serve for all the times of the year and for this important place—that in its whole structure it was too "private" and not spacious enough to enable the congregation to live within it. But it also seemed to us that within this event another is contained which possesses all of these qualities and which even became the space within which the Saint himself lived: that period when the Lord hangs bleeding on the cross. To be sure this, too, is a phase in the life of the Lord which ends after a time, but it is large enough to shelter whole days and years. It could step forward out of the whole and become for it a house, the congregation could live within it and there daily renew their sacrifice.

Once when we were requested to give an opinion on the suitability of a crucifix which a sculptor had made for the choir wall in a new church we met with an opposite situation. The crucifix had been objected to because of the great suffering represented in it. In itself, this was not a rare case. The Great War had not been over for long, and for the most part the people had experienced it in the image of the crucifixion. They found their own deeds and their own suffering expressed in the theme of the murder of God. A large number of such crosses, put up by able artists over the altar at the very heart of both old and new churches, bore witness that the lonely dying of Christ was present to the times. And thus these churches were utterly dedicated to this frightful mystery.

Actually there was little that could be said against this. Certainly the cross is inwardly "statuesque" enough even for this place. Indeed the sacred act, and life itself, stand always under its shadow. Nor did the protestations of the "bourgeois" of the spiritual life carry much weight, for to them the truth will always be foolishness—and assuredly, too, the work was not badly done. Despite everything the congregations did not find themselves expressed in these works and we believed that we saw the reason. Each age has its own particular calling which it must fulfill. This calling is so to speak its house, its living space, the vessel into which it pours its days and years. There have been times which really were placed beneath the cross, but for this time this was not so. Its true content was not death, but rather a wonderfully healing young life which budded in a thousand promises. The congregations could not endure living ever under the death of the Lord because this was not their task. Indeed, within the whole epoch this death had been only an episode. Death had passed through the time and here the right means had not been chosen to represent this passing by. Perhaps—as we once proposed in the course of building a church—a great crucifix could have been placed in the courtyard like a doorpost, the two arms stretching from wall to wall. The people would then have passed through this doorway. Or perhaps the hint provided by a very small cross placed on the altar would have been enough.

We have a very beautiful opportunity of observing, *in statu nascendi* as it were, the way a process sinks its roots and grows fast to a particular spot: the "Stations of the Cross." The idea of this old spiritual exercise is very simple. One goes along a path and on the way one observes the way of the Lord from Pilate to Golgotha. At the spot where a particular event took place one stands still for a little while to meditate upon it. Originally this was a usage of pilgrims and then it was brought back home where some mountain path was consecrated as the way of the cross. The individual places were marked by numbers or little pictures. This exercise was felt to be genuine liturgical representation and it was thought that the way of the cross is something eternal and that every Christian must go this way over and over again. In itself, it is indeed a way, a progress, and the stations upon it are events. But inasfar as the progress measured off a particular stretch of the way and inasfar as each of its events marked a particular place, progress became a stretch of way and event became place. The story took root, the periods and occurrences grew fast in the earth and gradually the little markings turned into statues. Many of these occurrences were particularly spacious and above these rose the Mounts of Olives, the chapels of the Mother of Sorrows, the Mounts of Calvary and the pilgrimage churches consecrated to the Holy Cross. Thus history was transcribed into architecture.

The exercise of the Way of the Cross shows how one event can step forth out of a whole act and become structure. Within the whole, the event is only a "period," but our architecture, our painting and our sculpture are indeed linked to the age. We even date the epochs according to their artistic styles.

An age builds its own form and this form is valid as long as the age endures.

Then the next age builds its form onto the first and through the milleniums the cathedral grows. It will go on being built until the end of time. Thus the Middle Ages built their great naves and meanwhile longed for the dome which was denied them until finally it was achieved when the new time came.

Such slow amplification of the beginning, such gradual increase in which each age adds its new part, is the right way, the way in which we can indeed gradually succeed in building world history. Each new addition lasts to that final day on which the church will be completely built. In this age-old cathedral the basic form of the sacred history desposits itself for all eternity.

And it is very obvious, too, that the Gothic cathedral does not merge completely with its own age—in part it towers into the whole. At the front of the high nave, which belongs completely to the epoch, stands the triptych. It is a tiny cathedral. According to the seasons of the sacred year it displays various occurrences and at the greatest occasion the whole body of history is unfolded as a shining order. And thus at least the most sacred spot takes part in the cathedral, reaching out from the form of the age into the fullness of sacred history. And then, too, round about the nave lie the chapels, with their many altars. They lie at the sides, but even so they are present. They serve the veneration of a particular event or of a particular saint. When one of the chapels awoke to its service, the lights were lit there and the people formed concentric rings about it; fixed seats were unknown, the position of the people was not predetermined and they were able to mark off their temporary space from the whole. Later on, when the lights had been put out, life moved into another space. These saints and these events were linked into the whole. Some particular part out of the whole was entrusted to each of them, and all of them together, people and destinies, made up the living body of history. All of history was a gathering of living events and of living men and women. Indeed, they could hardly think of the whole in any other way, it lived and they were allowed to serve it.

Once we tried to take up again the concept which was intended in the triptych. To this end we placed a table in the center of the design and the earth apportioned herself outward from it. The people could stand all around it or they could leave empty one or several of the wings of the building, all of which were directed toward the center; the priest could stand in front of the altar or behind it. Thus each of the great basic forms could be represented through the articulation of the people. The building would take some part, as it were, in the transformation of time's forms. This could be emphasized still further by the changing lighting and by the changing decoration of the space.

And lastly the building can live in the single day and in its swift transformation. The sun travels its path about the building, first the east side and then the west are bathed in light. Now this window lights up, now that, depending on the hour. When we plan the windows we should pay attention to this beautiful, quiet movement of the light and we should set down in them a continuous sequence of sacred words for the light to read out. How gloriously the day dies in the deep red of the rose windows of the early cathedrals, merging wholly into the final glow of the Father's love for his creatures! And how gloriously the blessed vision breaks in at last, out of the declining day!

PART IV
The Test

The Test

BEFORE THIS WORK comes to an end we must sum up once more what is meant with it.

It is intended to be a primer for church building—no more but also no less. And so it will be objected that it concerns only a few, only that small group which has to do with the architecture of churches.

This is true and false.

True it is that this book is strictly and intentionally limited to the art of building. Everything which has been said here holds true only for the building art and where this limit has been overstepped what has been said holds true only insofar as it serves to advance this art. But that to which we limit ourselves is broadly and seriously taken for what it is: the art which builds. If this art were concerned only with placing an already existing content in an attractive frame, with ornamenting it with fitting motifs and with expressing it in a pleasing form, then indeed all this would concern no one but a few experts. Our book would then have to look like all the others which one can buy: it would report on the requirements of the authorities, impart all sorts of practical experience, perhaps go over the building costs and give a few typical plans.

But it is exactly this which does not occupy us here. For we spoke about the building of something which does not yet exist and we asked how it might be built. It was about the building of the Church herself that we spoke. The art of building, as we meant it, is the creation of living form, and the church, as we meant it, is not merely a walled shelter, but everything together: building and people, body and soul, the human beings and Christ, a whole spiritual universe—a universe, indeed, which must ever be brought into reality anew. We meant the primal deed of building, the process in which church becomes living form.

This holy work is comparable to no other. It cannot be derived from contemporary art and its fashionable motifs nor from the aesthetic doctrines nor from social theories nor from cosmic myths. Rather is church building a work in its own right, bound strictly to its own meaning and with it exhausted. Church building is not applied theology nor is it the fulfillment of a liturgical purpose (and thus a chimera): it is "work which prays," work which is borne by the movement of grace. We develop an engine, a business organization or a strategical plan, not out of a superimposed motive, but out of their own inner law. That just as strictly a church must be developed wholly and in all its parts out of its own inner meaning, that is, out of prayer,—this is to us the meaning of "sacred objectivity."

The substance of all church building, its own meaning, sacred, irreplaceable and inexchangeable, is the living church. The "structure" is her "visibleness," so much so that the building itself, taken together with all its contents as a living unity, is the revealed form, the revealed structure of the Church. The teachings about church building, or better, leading to church building, are instruction in how the Church comes into being. And she is taken so seriously, so literally and above all so "visibly," that she can be written down in great "plans."

Building as we mean it—the forming of reality—is assuredly a work which takes its place among the other works of thinking, teaching, healing, ruling and so on. Therefore it is entrusted to a particular calling. But building is one of the true callings, one of those which ask the ultimate questions and whose work is total. The architect who builds is the vicar of all architectural reality. He gives visible form to that which erects itself secretly inside of men. But all are bound in duty to the building, all are involved in his total work—that the Church come into being ever and again, that the spiritual form be real, for this all are accountable. But one man makes manifest the form of the common spiritual structure and in his deed the rules and plans of sacred "edification" can be recognized. Therefore the building is the concern of all for it is an image of that first architecture which God himself works with his people—it is a true "symbol."

The number of true callings, of those which stand for an ultimate, irreducible attitude toward the world, is small; and among themselves they stand in a strict order. Each in its own way reaches to the innermost point of the world and together they form the ring. If one of them is neglected the others still have, in their way, whole world, but now there is a gaping hole in their order and the world becomes "one-sided." Yet this is exactly the case today. Theoretical knowledge—and this usually in accordance with the rules of science—has repressed the other callings. It takes up too much room.

Today almost all our books are out after knowledge. In reading them we pursue the clue of a train of thought and gradually we discover a result. Afterward we know something and as we recapitulate the knowing process we experience how knowing takes place at all. There is nothing to be said against this; such books are good in their way.

But to know means to have the things—we get rich by knowing. First the things are understood, we comprehend and define them and gradually they enter into us. Such books, if they are good, are of little help to the architect. They are not written for him since he is a different sort of man. He does not want to have the things, he constantly gives his very self to his works, he gives himself away. His whole hope is that many of his works will turn out well—and in this he is like all those who create, and like good parents, too, whose whole care is that their children may turn out well and who themselves grow old and worn out in the task. He, too, must know the things, but in a restrained way, without comprehending them. He must know whether this is a good loam, fit for the firing of bricks, whether this tree grew straight so that it can serve as a ridge-pole; he must know what he can expect of the men who work with him and where they will fail him; he must know what people need, he must know what different things can be used for and how they react, he must know the structure of the world and its laws and powers. But all his knowledge is of a practical sort. He sees all things in their openness and readiness, he sees in them potentiality. His knowledge is not therefore worse, not shallower than that of knowing people. But it is different. For him, to know means to unlock, to realize. He is full of tenderness, which means that he is full of a serious love for the details; and he recognizes the things at the heart, for what is to come into being will grow from the heart. Carefully he leaves the world at rest in herself, and he takes her into his hand, not to have her but to awaken her. His knowledge of the things is a hoping, sensing, dreaming knowledge. Only when the things unfold does he really recognize them. His knowledge of the things is different from that of the scholars. Scientifically he may make tremendous mistakes without, however, being deceived in the things themselves.

This good architect has his own particular way of speaking about the things. He names them and suddenly they are overflowing with possibilities. He speaks to them and they unfold. They become confiding and begin to move and to find their proper places almost by themselves. To speak as a builder means to speak "constructively." This speech is full of directing, encouraging expressions, of words which lay themselves under the things like helping hands. Today our books do not speak in this way—they speak in concepts. We have said nothing against conceptual knowing and we do not mean to say anything against the speech which is proper to it, but this speech is not good for building. Since knowledge itself is an internal work, it must of necessity lead away from building which is an external one. We can make either a building or a science out of the things but we cannot do both at once. In immuring the things and in knowing them, we exhaust their possibilities. This is indeed the reason why our literature bears so little

fruit: it is learned authorship, historical or aesthetic or theological or something else of the sort, but the words of the builder are lacking in it. We must
go very far back in order to find books which are edifyingly written, to find
good experienced books for the doing, books which honestly and in the face
of eternity take great care and pains about the question of what we should
do. For this is the highest concern of all edifying writings—and truly it
stands on the same plane with the final questions of the knowing intellect; its
concern is with the ultimate effecting as the concern of the mind is with the
ultimate knowing. (Only blissfully bewildered mystics confuse the two in
the first intoxication of a true form or a new insight.) What a corruption
when modern metaphysicists seek to make such questions contemptible!
Indeed, the question was once fully put: "What must we do to be saved?"
All other questions of the creative life are shadows and effects of this one
final query. When scholars ask how God may be proved—which means
when they ask how the way of knowledge may become so deeply embedded
in the truth that in the end God is manifest—and when the architect asks
how he may begin his work and carry it out in such a way that it may
succeed as God's work, then both are doing what is right, both are seeking
salvation, and out of this highest salvation their whole work will turn out
to be good. But neither takes precedence over the other. And that is the
reason why we take the question of church building so seriously. In the
realm of the creative it stands at the place where the question concerning
the knowledge of God stands in the realm of scholarship. This is the primal
question in our calling, no other can replace it and no one can relieve us of
it. We can do it justice only when we remain completely within the realm of
the architect. And when we speak we may only ask how our works may turn
out to be true works,—and this regardless of whether we are understood or
misunderstood. (And the prospect of being misunderstood is the greater,
since the species of books for doing has died out; there are inquiries into
the beautiful, into art, but there are no longer teachings which show us how
our work may succeed beautifully.)

And so the old teachings about the good works would have to be renewed.

Now we hear the objection which we have long awaited: can there even be such a thing as a book which teaches doing? Can right doing—which of course should always be a spontaneous and a new doing, too—can this right doing be taught? And if such a teaching does exist, can it be imparted through a book?

In a book we can record experience, make notes of all the things which are valid for every work and which must be kept in mind in every case, we can provide a list of constants and obviously we can also give a good description of the materials, in keeping with the matter at hand—and certainly the knowledge of these unchanging things is also indispensable to right doing. But that which is not unchanging, that which should be effected spontaneously and in freedom, can this be written down ahead of time? Will this not hurt the secret of creation or lock it out? May we dare to write a book which actually intends, in the strictest sense, to teach?

In itself the assertion that art cannot be taught is nonsense. Of course we can teach it. But we cannot let it be learned by heart like a material which is simply finished and ready for us. Art's lesson is given in the actual process of achievement and the teaching of art is to be found where master and pupil overcome all of the difficulties of a task together, and where the pupil, becoming utterly one with the teaching master and being taken up completely into the inner space of the process, is permitted to accompany him through all the dangers of miscarriage up to the successful solution.

This book, however, is a printed and published instruction. It does not know its pupil and his particular case and it cannot go with him the one, indispensable way. It can only say the things in general; but the things are such that they possess no "in general." Nothing definite can be established about them and no general instructions can be given for them. There are no formulas as to how a man must conduct himself when, hoping for the gift of new life, he dares to venture into the void. Nothing more can grow where the germinating power of a process has been used up in definitions.

This difficulty is not new. The old books for right doing which we have mentioned were written in the face of this same difficult condition. They, too, were meant to be books for the teaching of work, indeed for the teaching of the greatest and loftiest work: instructions in the blessed life. And nevertheless they accomplished their task. Therefore we must link the new discipline of books for doing onto their severed tradition.

Most of these books for work are collections of restrained guidance. They do not in the least attempt to regulate life by dividing it up into a system of possible cases each of which then receives a particular recipe; that would lead us to the Chinese or simply into the formal etiquette of the polite, and the books would be reference books. A good book for doing must not work out the final solution at all, for then the life which would come afterward would be only a copy of it—the book must keep back the solution. Each working-out can thrive only at its own moment, in the particular grace of this right point of time. Therefore the book of history contains the only valid collection of models—there are no such things as solutions above and beyond history. A moving historical model teaches us how true growth succeeds and this encourages us to our own work. Therefore every good teaching for work must show the great, model solutions—and it must show them not scientifically but encouragingly, so that they may serve, not as models to be copied but rather as prototypes. Indeed this work, too, is conceived in this way. Only an unmistakable radicalism can seek to keep the careful study of the history of art out of the practical instruction.

In addition to the part which contains information about the materials and to the second part which gives the historical teachings, the good book for work consists of a multitude of instructions some of which are perhaps no more than a scanty word or a gesture of the hand. They are set side by side and we read through them with the thought that all this does not concern us, until we hit upon the particular case, the present one, our own. This single word of counsel comes strangely to life and we feel almost as if it had come just now at the right hour from a knowing and providential power. In this the good book for work is like creation itself which is full of graces, full of seeds and possibilities, each of which is awaiting the right man at the right hour to set it free. This good book would be the world herself, trans-

formed utterly into her readiness. The book would have to be in some way
complete lest someone whose particular case were missing should remain
without counsel. It must be complete, be it that the instructions really do
expand to embrace the universe, or be it that their inner order is of such an
encouraging incompleteness that the reader, whose own case is not expressly
foreseen, is led to invent the appropriate solution for himself. Eckhart's
"Talks of Instruction" are of this kind. Thomas à Kempis' book is constructed in this way also—its short instructions, apparently so accidental
and disconnected, are yet bound mutually to one another by the integrity
of a life which, ripening through experience, has come to wisdom. This book
which calls itself an imitation of the Lord and which nevertheless scarcely
mentions him, teaches a far more genuine imitation than many contemporary books whose aim is to copy the holy story as literally as possible in the
present. The good workbook is built not according to a pattern but according to an economy of life: it offers the things as germ. Here there is no more
looking up, the book opens by itself. In former times readers believed so
implicitly in this creative secret that they opened the books blindfolded and
thought that the right counsel would then of itself be found lying on the
opened page.

Whether this book is a good book for work?

In any case it is conceived in the manner of the old books for teaching. It
builds itself up out of a number of "plans" which join together into a whole,
and this, too, is again a "plan." These "plans" are not model designs since
they leave off at exactly the point where the decisions would have to fall out
of which they could become "concrete." We may realize them in many ways
but they themselves persevere short of realization in a state of quiet reserve.
Only in this or that particular one of their many possible interpretations
would they turn into true designs. This essay is not a collection of models.
We could not even attempt such a collection for now as we write, here, in
this year, we do not have all historical situations at hand—we have only this
particular one or that. Far more are the "plans" intended to be genuine

"instructions" imparted in the language of architecture. They exist in pre-reality.

With the "plans" we introduce something new into the doctrines of architecture and we must contrast the new with the known lest they be confused. First of all, our "instructions" are not model designs; secondly, they are not specifications; thirdly, they are not parts of an architectural "canon" and, fourthly, they are not "formulas."

The Specifications

Our "instructions" are not specifications.

The particular directions in connection with a building which are called the "specifications" are a description of the task in numbers and measurements. They specify the stipulations for the building down to the last detail, they tell for how many people it is to be built, what costs may be incurred and so on. The specifications subtract from the task its concreteness and they express this concreteness by means of a certain type of numbers and signs. These serve to separate what is concrete from what would be possible and they stand at the opposite pole from the kind of numbers and signs which name form and rhythm. These latter are final for the form as such; the former, however, help the form to enter reality for the first time. $2\pi r$ is the circle. Here 2π is always valid and "r" holds the place open for that which changes in each particular case. But only $2\pi a$ is an actual circle within history. These "a's", extracted from the entire building, are the specifications. Today we know that giving the specifications is itself a part of the work of designing, for it is the specifications which give to life its ground plan. And we work out the specifications very carefully when we are confronted by a concrete task for what we seek above all else today is the new ground plan for life itself. But obviously this book contains no "a" at all—cannot contain it—and therefore it is not a book of specifications.

The Canon

Or is this 2π, this "type" which is incarnated in actual building, this pure form—is it exactly this which the plans should specify? Should they perhaps provide that canon of building which would interpret the timeless meaning of the architectural forms? And should all of them together perhaps yield a doctrine of "sacred measure" (Lenz)?

The doctrine of measure and of the eternal meaning of geometry is something very great and it was the trade secret of the medieval masons. In the numbers and figures watch was kept over the world's profound meaning and this meaning was then realized architecturally. In the course of time this ancient teaching fell into decay. Fragments of it continued to be handed down for a long time but its over-refined rules no longer yielded results, and they failed to stand the test of time. The doctrines of form had lost their relation to the world and were reduced to a compendium of historical motifs, until at last these, too, were laid aside as life itself brought forth new and genuine forms.

This was not the fault of the teachings themselves. In the course of his work every serious artist comes upon the fact that the forms themselves have an ultimate meaning. The development was more a result of the times which were blind and did not see how the world, filled with color and tone, stands everywhere in form. And so it is natural that today as our senses reawaken, the doctrine of form reawakens, too. In certain places this doctrine is already being taught and practised once again. In the beginning it originated in opposition to the excesses of functionalism and to the rank growth of constructional teachings connected with it. It defended the sublimity of the form itself against the utilitarianism of the construction. This doctrine taught that form has an "eternal meaning" in itself, and the collection of these forms was supposed gradually to yield the "canon," a sort of dogma of architecture. The construction should carry and sustain the exalted, purposeless form.

Thus the concern about the doctrine of form, which in itself is a right concern, became bound to a classically-aesthetic conception of form. This canon was a doctrine of empty dimensions into which one poured the stuff of the world—forming meant the minting of dumb material. This teaching based itself on the sculptural form and at least it was able to provide classicistic buildings. The architecture of antiquity is not false. Aside from the fact that it was once historical, it represents an eternal possibility in building, and that which is archaic in it, its symmetry and static quality, can be changed. Therefore a canon which is derived from it is not false and yet it is narrow. It is limited to the validity of this "sculptural form," and like it, this canon is a matter of feeling and taste.

The Formula

As the old canon faded, a new race of numbers arose which designated the form of pure function. The lineal growth of dead nature was represented in the growth of mathematical progressions and the movements of the things found their image in the mathematical formula. With it the world's own movement could be controlled: in new and magnificent structures men mastered nature whose formula they had got hold of. And so the Greek form vanished.

These new numbers define the insides of the things and the work which they do is the work of the "grasping hand." They say nothing about the meaning of the things, blindly they do a blind work. The formula, as we know it today, is method without content; the work of technology does not itself see what it creates. Technology is without countenance, without feeling, without hearing. But her method is potent and nature produces mighty forms in response to her spell. A well-spring of new and primal form has burst forth. Where genuine form appears today at all it is almost always of "technical" origin. Nature yields herself to the form of the new doing and this she would never do had the new speech not touched her in her very depths.

As science "grasps" the things, technology moves them. Concept and ma-

chine are brothers—and this is the root to which we must trace all the many
attacks made against them, attacks which so often seem senseless and which
are so often unrealistically formulated. But indeed the concept broadens,
the "world of forms" grows on to it and gradually out of a comprehended
world grows a world which we perceive and recognize. Technology could
change in the same way. We can but dimly sense what great things would
come to pass were the whole creative human being to enter into "technical"
work—to enter into it not in order to decorate it but in order to bring to
bear in serious work the creative power of the feeling hand, of the seeing
eye, of the hearing ear, of the whole moving and effecting body. Such serious work would still be—or would be for the first time—truly valid and
effective work. This other technology—actually it would be a new architecture, the heiress of the Gothic—is our greatest hope. Promising beginnings are already at hand: now we are commencing to "see" technology and
what we see is a primeval forest of forms clothing the earth. These forms are
proven in hard tests, they are powerful, wild and primary, and unfortu-
nately they are neglected—but they are real. The fact that we see this forest
of forms is, however, the beginning of a true liberation from within—and
this liberation has nothing to do with the decorations of the handicrafters and
the sociologists even though these, too, have sometimes been referred to as an
emancipation. And is not this liberation already at hand in the great and oft
misunderstood doctrine of the new architecture?

In this liberation the true rule for work—that rule in which actual growth
is prefigured, that rule which is the indication of genuine organic form—
would grow out of the formula. We hope for this formula-widened-into-rule
and we see in it the coming "northern canon." If it succeeds, the other
teachings about form will pale in comparison, they will drift to the periphery and will seem almost like a tie connecting us to some remote archaeological state of our thought. For the new architect the "technical" form
would be something which is spanned between heaven and earth and which
stands ready for everything. In his form he raises the lowest to the highest:
he builds cathedrals out of the forms of necessity. He believes that the high-

est things and the lowest things can find room in its form. Out of necessity he forges a weapon with which he enters the inner battlefield. He does not hide the dangerous inside in an attractive frame, rather does he try to master it. He does not design the things in accordance with superimposed ideas of "pure form," his fight is rather for the inner space. For him the destiny of the world is decided deep within, work is for him an inner effecting, or, better, an effecting which moves from the inside to the outside.

This is not a utopia, it is everyday reality. It is proven in the great cities which call forth the movement of traffic, in buildings which bring to expression the technical form, and in all the many machines in which men sit not as workers but as "drivers."

Those who keep watch over the classical form oppose the new work. To them its nakedness is painful. The inner form of the world must be veiled in a free façade like life itself—life, which, counseled by its own structural wisdom, never shows itself as a skeletal apparatus but always in beautiful disguise. At bottom life is gruesome and impossible: it calls for masks. To grant them is not cowardice and certainly not falsehood but rather a courageous "yes" to life as it really is. If this matter comes to discussion at all, then it is rather the others who are untruthful, those who wish to carry out life in open inwardness, for what they claim is not even possible: it contradicts the natural order. Classical form seeks to serve life benignly and wisely, true to that law in accordance with which life actually is built; and it believes that it may therefore claim to be the truer form. It knows that inwardly the things are different and more difficult. But the fact that it knows this and nevertheless continues to maintain its position, shows the peculiar mortal bravery of this classical culture at her most advanced outposts.

First we must reach an understanding about what is actually meant in this discussion, reply the "technologists." A form of pure inwardness is simply a chimera, like a sphere without a surface. Everything in this world comes to an end somewhere and where it ends lies a boundary; and this is something quite different from the inner space. Of course there have been a few high-flown people who wanted to manage with pure inwardness alone. The painters of recent decades, whose lovable courage led them to try everything once, showed us such forms, puddles of color on the point of dissolving. More liable to suspicion were the cloud-like pictures of Anthroposophical artists. Really, say the technologists, it is not nice to think *them* capable of such nonsense. Obviously the real question here is something quite different, namely whether the outside of the things should be the form of the inside's boundary—as is most clearly the case in the stereometric bodies—or whether it comes from somewhere else, out of an entirely different world, and may simply be laid over the top of the inside. A construction can be effected completely logically and in every part from the inside out in one single movement of form. The question here was whether we should demand this. The difference between surface and content is well known to the technologists from their study of physics; they know that the things have a surface and that different rules apply there from those which apply inside. They know the surface as that front where life throws up its rampart and they know the great transformation which a content undergoes when it draws near to its end. To them the surface is the outermost proclamation of the content. Their form is not inwardness set up on display but rather that boundary which the inside erects against the world. The peculiar honesty of this their form is that it confesses to this condition of bordering and does not attempt to disguise it with something utterly different; whatever originates in this way is an organic structure, purified to its very depths, within an ordered fullness and toward the outside not a façade but a front. Indeed it has turned out that the exterior is often more independent than it seemed to be in the beginning and that the pure shell construction remains an extreme exception. But that the boundary is the correct "behavior" of the inside when it reaches the outside: this is the decisive point.

The Instruction

Here the discussion ends. Indeed, both sides are right. One can work like a sculptor or like an engineer and both methods are fit for the highest. Hard by the crucial threshhold stand the extreme cases: the anatomical structure whose form is nothing but the place where a content comes to an end, and the stiff packaging where the content can no longer even be perceived through the sculptured form. Thus there can be two types of the doctrine of form, one which feels and one which grasps. Our hope, however, is that they may permeate one another and then together govern a work which will be accomplished neither by the feeling hand nor by the grasping hand but rather by the entire living body—a doctrine based in whole and living form.

Our concern here, however, has nothing to do with a doctrine of form or a doctrine of "sacred measure"—our concern is rather living teaching of which the rule is a part.

Doctrines of form are glorious when we discover them. He who has been blind grows intoxicated when he suddenly sees how the world stands in form. But if the doctrines are at once at hand we find them useful and necessary but at bottom disappointing. They provide a rule for life but they do not awaken it. They are empty form. Even "sacred measure" is an empty phrase: it holds true either in a completely metaphorical sense, for example when one thinks that the world—the world which is by nature measured world, inasfar as it is so—is sacred and one thus imagines that God occupies himself with geometry; or it holds true in a completely private sense, in that one thinks it particularly saintly to keep to a modest middle-of-the-road; or it is simply an obscure archaeological phrase. In the last analysis all rule is a modest matter—it outlines the repetitive forms which life assumes, not more. Forms permeate the structure of the world and even the formlessness of the amorphous creatures is in its way form. Yet at bottom the rules say something only about the condition of the things. They make a declaration of position in the river of time. To be a ball does not mean to be this or that, angel or atom, but only to experience this balled condition at the moment. But that which passes through all these conditions and maintains itself amongst them is not the ball, which will be cast aside again when its time is over, but rather a being which possesses all these different conditions and which outlasts them. What kind of a being this may be, how it may be awakened and called into life—about all this the doctrine of form says nothing. All form is blind condition and even the most proven rule provides only blind procedure, leaving creation completely free. Procedure does not say what should be created, but only how this thing which is to be created may logically be built—in the event that it actually should be created. Nor does the "technical" rule provide more, and in it the northern danger appears once again: the danger of setting out with empty method on the journey into the void.

In the "plans" a doctrine of form for the sacred can be discovered since it is contained in them. But in that case one would see only what is general in them, one would examine them with scientific eyes. They are, however, more. Were they nothing but this, they would accomplish for the work of architecture what scientific method accomplishes for knowledge—not more. In scholarship the difficult question arises as to how one who is steeped in scholarly doctrine may impart the truth. The corresponding question arises here: how can we give the general rules for work in such a way that they may awaken living doing?

How does new work originate at all?

Obviously it is not "the union of wordless impulse with brilliant ideas"—this is falsely observed: the thrice false myth of a formless depth, a lifeless form and the wedding of the two. It is not in some dark stream of formless world-impulse that the artist, diving deep, encounters his new idea; and it is not the world of forms into which he raises it up for the first time and in which he carries it out. This deep, dark primeval current flowing beneath the visible world is far more the eternal stream of the germs of the things —of the things which take place above where it is light. Those things which flow within this stream are not formless drives—they are germs, possible contents and possible forms bound inseparably into one, the seed of history. Even this first intuition to which the artist weds himself is not a dumb impulse for which he seeks the fitting form above—rather is it a *form* which occurs to him, a work which overcomes him.

New life kindles itself on older life. Life is sown, borrowed, transplanted, it is handed on in a thousand ways, but never as an amorphous form or generalization, always and only as a living coal. The living body of history grows out of the living seed of older deeds. Only a teaching which proffers the germ of work uninjured is a teaching to true work. A doctrine which insists on form without imparting the glimmering spark is empty and leaves its listeners cold.

The great events are like ancient trees about which a young forest grows. They themselves are finished and belong to history. But ever and again the finished event forces forth the fruitful new beginning, a shoot which may be transplanted. It bears it as a ripe fruit, its whole structure is covered over and over with new beginning: one great bewitchment. But it is ever so—life must once more grow small and withdraw into the withholding germ before it becomes new. The things must change utterly into their potentiality if they are to grow up once more as something new. First they must plunge deep into the river of heritage which flows beneath all history. But it is the things themselves, held in suspense as germ, which flow within this river.

This, indeed, is what fruitful teaching gives: the seeds of things. The teaching goes to the great happening and transforms it into instruction; and then it proffers this instruction. Fruitful teaching relieves the event of the accidental quality of its having happened at a certain particular moment and it gives insight into what was actually intended with it. Teachings set the form of growth in relief as living rule and they transpose the event into its potentiality; but teaching does not divide up the happening nor does it subtract anything from it—it leaves it whole.

The "plans" are intended to be such instruction. The form in which they exist is not easy to understand for one must first get used to it. They are genuine happening which has withdrawn utterly into its potentiality, which has become wholly seed and beginning and which waits, not to be copied down again, but to grow up once more as new event, which waits to be chosen out of the profound knowledge of its appointed destiny and to be led high in that true succession which is born of freedom. And so the plans stand in the true tradition, in the only tradition there is, bound living into future and past, into the changing generations of history. And, indeed, in the last analysis, there is only one fruitul canon: true life.

In the Life of the Lord the great model of sacred architecture is forever given us. Church architecture is not cosmic mythology—rather is it the representation of Christian life, new embodiment of the spiritual. And thus it is the imitation of the Lord in the language of building and with the materials of architecture. It is easy to understand that Pinder doubted whether our time was capable of sacral building, lacking as it does the valid mythology—he drew the conclusion that architecture itself is denied us. Perhaps this mythology is lacking. Or perhaps it is not. If it is lacking, we can build no temples (and Pinder really meant temples)—and this pains us, for temples are necessary. But he who wishes to build a church needs no myth as his basis. He must, however, make his decisions in a Christian way. He must believe that God's son became man and wrought and suffered and he must believe that since that time there has been but one "sacred measure": not the Pythagorean number, not some magic spell, but rather the life of the Lord in body and in history, because God found it good to show in him and to impart in him the form at the root of sacred happening. Sunk deep into the history of the world, this form grows up out of it again a thousandfold. The architect must believe that God has revealed his own being in the sacred history and he must believe that therefore even God himself is not something or other but rather a clear form, and also that, glorifying him, one gives him back his own message when, in the building of a church, one forms creation to sacred body. He must believe that there is truth in the fantastically bold word about the birth of God among men—and likewise in that other word that man is the measure of all things: he is, but only because he has been measured by the measure of God. The congregation, the meeting of the individuals, is also measured thus. It is not a formless mass, a filling liquid, rather is it elemental form, and its structural measure corresponds to that of the individual body so that it, too, may be called sacred body.

Here we cannot name all the consequences which thus develop for architecture, but they lead far afield from the aesthetical ideas. Architecture, too, towers above the individualistic accident, is absolute coherence and given form—and again, not just any form but rather the great form of God. Thus the church building is an exalted song composed out of individual and congregation, out of space, construction and the act of worship, into all of which the same eternal measure is sunk deep. Church building is made possible only through the prior measurement of all elements according to the same measure and where this exalted song rings out, a church has been built.

We have now exhausted that which is teachable in the matter of church building. Our teaching, too, ends at the brink where all things end, in the face of the eternal abyss. Whether that answer will be given which then succeeds in true building no book of teaching can say. Grace cannot be insisted on, cannot be forced, there is no procedure which procures it. The slightest thought of this sort frightens it away. For the building art this is a particularly difficult truth which must constantly be born in mind. For indeed this art erects the felicitous moment to lastingness, deposits the infinite joy in great forms, forms the successful method to rule. How strongly is she tempted to make a method, perhaps thrice successful, into a magic formula!

An honest teaching limits itself to that which is man's teachable work. It says that church building is the great form of surrender, the work of hands which open, sacred inaction. It is that work which grows ever smaller, gradually ceasing, that work in which man grows ever weaker, until, empty to the dregs, he stands at the brink before God. He gives himself up to God because there is nothing else left for him to do; but it does not occur to him —such a thought would be the subtlest perversion—that all this, the gradual cessation of his own hopes and the final surrender, could be a method for arriving at good works. He surrenders himself because he is hemmed in and because this leap is the only thing left him. The teaching can tell in which direction the road goes which leads there and it can say that all to whom it was given to achieve the very great things have gone this way. But the teaching cannot guarantee that this time they will be achieved again. It accompanies man up to the end and teaches him how to build the forms of surrender. Our book ends where all teaching must end: before the newness of grace. And the speech of teaching, too, subsides as the bring draws nearer, growing mute in that great stillness in which all creatures hearken to the Lord.

Is there then any sense in planning churches? If the only thing the workers can honestly do is to guide all created things into the form of their surrender? A building is home and shelter, but that which is demanded here is misery and exile.

No, in the great and real sense there is indeed little purpose for by ourselves we can build no churches: that, God must do. But far beneath the exalted realm of true architecture lies that other area where houses rise as temporary structures which are little more than needy dug-outs or scanty shelters. Such emergency buildings are the only possible accomplishments of men before God, waiting-rooms before his threshhold. They confess to the infinite need and they wait until God himself transforms it. This is the honorable way to build churches: before God begins his work.

This is not meant puritanically. We believe that God does not leave his people alone and that he really does give the answer ever and again. Only we do not wish the workmen to make themselves independent and to wall themselves off from the great and true achieving. Certainly everything is here made dependent upon grace, but is this so strange? Has not God already based the natural enduring of humanity upon the natural miracle of love, upon this miracle which no reason can compute or fathom? What need have we to be afraid if he has based humanity's eternal enduring solely upon the sacred miracle of his own love, upon a love which ever and again takes mercy upon the transiency of life and renews it through holy words?

Is not this, too, a part of that mute knowledge which all creative men possess and which nevertheless is written in no book—the knowledge that the worldly works, too, where they are great and new, stem from such failure and that God reserves them for himself? When God intends a new work with the world he calls on men and lets them begin bravely. But little by little he leads them into adversity. The works begin to miscarry and in the end the people stand before the Lord with empty hands and bitter hearts. They do not understand why he did this to them: was his call not clear?

Did not his grace bless the work so very visibly in the beginning and even later on, and did they not work and toil even beyond their strength? Why did he, the Almighty, break this small and honest work to bits? We may not judge harshly. Even saints have fought to the last for their human happiness and have harshly accused God, saying that he should leave them their little spot of green earth and the few simple things which he promised them when he created them as men. And perhaps when God sees that the people only become bitter he does not even go to the very end, but rather keeps them in the provisional stage of the small joys and comforts. This may be average human fate. But perhaps many things would turn out greater if men did not let themselves be borne by God's pity alone, if they did not place so many little preliminary works between themselves and their great appointed destiny but instead had the courage to go thither where their highest call leads them: to foster the intended annihilation, to surrender themselves to the incomprehensible movement and quietly to await its desire. In the end what it purposes is indeed the great and unexpected good, the unawaited succeeding. That which is new in the world comes straight from God at the moment when it is no longer hoped for; this is the mystery of true and sacred failure.

There is still something to consider. This need is sacred need. God effects even the forms of surrender. The first impulse to carry out the movement is given by him, grace causes the first step, the second, the third and finally the last. And that which comes there is not a world which has fallen away from God: it is his own holy child coming home to him.